Failing for Jesus

– CHRIS GRUMMITT –

An environmentally friendly book printed and bound in England by
www.printondemand-worldwide.com

This book is made entirely of chain-of-custody materials

www.fast-print.net/store.php

FAILING FOR JESUS (SECOND EDITION)

First published 2009 also by Fast-Print Publishing

A catalogue record for this book is available from the British Library

ISBN 978-178035-794-2

First published 2014 by
FASTPRINT PUBLISHING
Peterborough, England.

Failing for Jesus

Contents

Prologue: The Reasons

This extraordinary tale of miracles and mayhem in the front line trenches of spiritual warfare in Africa was naively laid down in 2006 and has been subjected to a rewrite and important update, which underscores both the cost and ongoing success of such a ministry.

The book has only one purpose and that is to encourage those who may consider that there is more to Christian discipleship than attending Church and a house-group, but there is warning for those who may be complacent. A thorough read of the New Testament will confirm this warning to be valid, as there appears to be very little understanding within the church as to what constitutes personal mission. However, there is no attempt to suggest that a bag should be packed and a ticket booked to enter the fray in some foreign field. God may require this but the truth is if discipleship is declared, and the name of Jesus is on the lips of the believer, then the mission field is all around. The Bible is quite clear on what will happen when we have to stand before our Lord and give an account and all quotations supporting this are taken from the NIV version for simplicity.

Jesus teaches us what to expect will happen if we are ignorant. If He, by grace, gives us salvation in order to live forever with him as co-heirs, then we are not meant to belittle or ignore it. He says in the book of John, in Chapter14, that if we love him then we must keep his commandments; the most important being to bring the Gospel to others.

'Go into all the world and preach the good news to all creation.' (Mark 16:15)

If He commands then surely we must obey?

As I have said the mission field is all around and we can obey Jesus or we can keep our mouths shut. We can tell people we are Christians or we can make excuses for our peculiar belief. We can stand up for justice and against unrighteousness or we can go with the flow of public opinion and ideology, even though it may be against the teachings of God. That is our choice; that is how it has been forever and our Saviour will never interfere with whatever we want to do. He forever gives us choice. What we refuse to do others will carry out.

We must realise exactly what is written in The Good Book regarding these commandments in order that we can stand on the fateful day and deliver a favourable report to Jesus. In return he does not ask us to succeed but to persevere and overcome.

We will fail often and that is why book was entitled '*Failing for Jesus.*' My original publisher immediately turned down the book because he said no one would want to read about failure, completely missing the

Biblical truth of the matter for God declares that even our righteous acts are but filthy rags in Isaiah 64:6. The publisher would not even take a read of the manuscript. How sad.

The alternative to obeying commandments of Jesus during our 'Christian' walk is to say that all these works are unnecessary. This school of thought believes that no activity will have any bearing on whether we will get into heaven or not, as we are saved by grace and that is simply all that is required. If this appears to be common knowledge I can assure anyone that, even so, it is a lie. Our salvation can never be obtained through works, but the witness that we are on the path to salvation will be evident by the works we will carry out. James points out in his book, showing that if we claim to have faith then there will only be one outcome.

'Show me your faith without deeds, and I will show you my faith by what I do.'
(James 2:18)

It is true that the gift of salvation is free by grace and undeserved because of our foul nature, and also true that Jesus enables the door to be opened when he said from the cross 'It is finished,' but to say there is no cost attached is undeserving. It is Jesus who says we are to deny ourselves and pick up our cross daily if we want to follow him. Ergo, we are not to live in a lap of luxury and do nothing, so do we really want to cheapen that walk to Calvary and say nothing is expected from us in return? The following scripture will be a shock to those who have never realised its import.

'Then the righteous will answer him. 'Lord when did we see you hungry and feed you, or thirsty and give you something to drink? When did we see you a stranger and invite you in or needing clothes and clothe you? When did we see you sick, or in prison and go to visit you?" The King will reply, 'I tell you the truth, whatever you did for one of the least of these bothers of mine, you did for me.'
(Matthew 25: 37-40)

It is plainly transparent that this is the judgement list as tabulated by Jesus himself. There can be no argument it is the template by which we will all be measured, Christian or not. I will leave it to the reader to decide whether this commandment can be met in kind or whether Jesus meant that this should be carried out by practice. I made my decision after becoming a Christian, 'devouring' my Bible and accepting His commands and His will for me. In the end it cost me dearly. Comfortingly, the price that has to be paid is predicted in the Bible, as are the gift from God, particularly where He promises to be with his people even to the end of the age. He teaches us to accept both and live a life counting everything as pure joy.

I have written this book because I was simply told to do so by The Lord during a conversation I had with dear Christian friends, when I was recounting an incident that took place in Africa. A voice came into my head which said "You will write these things down". These encounters in Africa still stir emotions even thirty years later but now He would require others to know. Sometimes I look back in awe when studying the notes I took during my ministry when I have to wonder why it is under the most trying of circumstances I still believe. I have only to pick up this book to immediately recollect: "Yes Lord I rode with you for a wonderful season and it was good."

My fervent wish is that this book is treated in the same way. It is the story of how a very loosely nominal but totally disobedient businessman in Britain was led into a ministry by Jesus, which could never have been imagined without evoking scorn and ridicule amongst family and friends. It is the story of a family who after intervention by The Holy Spirit, endured separation and who went off to darkest Africa, suffering losses, plagues, persecution, illness and finally apparent failure that nearly destroyed all concerned. Through it all though there was His magnificent glory.

I will tell the truth as seen through my eyes as a first hand witness to the works of the Lord. No punches are pulled over mentioning individuals or the establishments, they represented whether they be government or Church. The book will give an insight into an incredible world of evil where the roaring Lion prowls around looking for someone, or something to devour. (1 Peter 5.8) and where sin increased, grace increased all the more. (Romans 5:20)

The book contains heartbreak and tells of the deprivations and the tribulations that would be encountered. It talks about the missionary and his calling, his attitude, strengths and sadly many failures. A season is described in which, simply because there were no other means of help available in the most awful circumstances, people cried out to The Lord and were actually heard. But, it is not a comfortable book for those who do not believe in signs and wonders accompanying the preaching of the word. (Mark 16:16-18) Even though this may be so, I still beg that the book be read so that belief may enter the heart.

If there are any embellishments I ask for indulgence as they would be born out of the need to remember, when either using the frailty of human memory or zeal, but they will be slight and will have nothing to do with His work. Like many parts of the Bible this book concerns failure. However we cannot judge what The Lord considers is good and bad, but only be led to our respective goals. In my case very few 'believed' when I arrived and very few 'believed' when I left, but the experience changed my life and that of others forever.

The book is about a small country in West Africa; a place where I was called to and where all my hopes and aspirations seemed to founder; a memory for which there seemed to be no answers and no release. This, after my forced departure which tugged at my heart strings every time a guilty thought entered my head and every time a kind person enquired as to my state of health. It was a place I was forced to turn my back on, yet in my mind and heart I could never leave. It became a place I could never go back to unless to risk years of imprisonment, yet I had deserted those who were closest to me.

Back in Britain I continued to deteriorate in mind and body until one wonderful day when the Lord released me from the burden of unnecessary guilt, by sending me a friend with a word of knowledge. Prior to this it took a considerable effort for me to extricate myself from the tremendous sense of loss and the disorientation of being back in isolation. When disaster strikes, and when it is associated with the Lord's work, there is an immediate and overwhelming sense of loss and grief, even if the recipient of all this pain manages to maintain a sense of balance throughout the trauma. It is a feeling that friends, dependants, relatives, benefactors and most of all Jesus, have been let down in an inexplicable way. If any reading this book have been through a similar experience please note there is always absolution available. The important fact to remember is that He knows we are weak and frail, but still loves us. He will never let us despair.

It was only time and the support of family, close friends, and above all a steady healing through communication with Jesus that the balance was restored. The Lord, through a personal relationship, can impart to the one who is hurt the value of the work that was assigned. It is *only* the Lord who enabled me to motivate myself to plough on regardless. He taught me how my missionary days in Africa were glorious by any standards, and made me realise that I was made wiser through the ordeal and that this strength would be required for other ministries and trials that were to follow, and follow they did.

During it all I learned a depth of compassion and understanding that I would have considered beyond myself. I experienced the inner torment of the soul that screams out for the love of God, for so many. I learnt to dump all my prejudices simply because I witnessed first-hand that God chose to pour out his power indiscriminately, to black and white, Christian and non-Christian. I learned to boast only in the Cross, and to defend its salvation in the most extreme circumstances, taking on the devil's agents in their own backyard. I learned, to my utter surprise, to be respected for my belief, particularly when I chose to associate myself with those often considered life's drop outs. Finally, I learned to bear persecution and be almost hated by some of those who I considered friends and brothers, by going to a place where it would not hurt at all; the arms of Jesus.

If all that is contained in this book is failure, then we maybe we all fail and in doing so learn to be utterly dependent on God. However let us not dwell on this but find out just how the Lord answered a particular cry from my heart, which eventually led to my family being transported from extreme comfort in a Suffolk village to a steamy and hostile environment in West Africa.

I have a duty to protect myself and my family as well as friends and all those connected with this ministry. The reason will become evident as the book unfolds. Most of those mentioned I would love with open arms. Some, I love with the love that Jesus put in me and others I have prayed for, being my persecutors. The names of people and places have been changed and God willing I hope one day to return, not as a tourist, but for a reason and possibly another season.

Chapter 1: Miserable Burden

The telephone rang in the hallway. Reluctantly, I strode out of the living room and picked it up. "Hello Chris this is Charles...Charles Rose." My fragility is dangerously challenged; mind awash with conflicting emotions. Back to Africa and the nightmare of failure, and now my old friend threatens to open the floodgates memory.

"Charles Rose." was repeated again until I falteringly acknowledged the call.

I came to my senses and welcomed the caller who I had not seen for some time and whom my family had entertained in our African bungalow many months previously. It transpired that Charles, a former volunteer in Africa, was passing through Suffolk where we were living and could, if we so wished, spend a Sunday talking over old times. He was informed that we would be glad to see him and that he was welcome to accompany us to church in the morning, and later have some lunch together. Charles enthused before he rang off however I was left wondering whether this was such a good idea. I was just about stabilised and was learning to stop abusing myself with bad memories and here was Charles totally unaware that he could set me back weeks. What was my friend Charles going to stir up tomorrow? What new horror could be dragged out of the recesses of my memory? Nevertheless, I hoped some sort of catharsis could possibly take place, yet dreading its process, but not with the sight of seeing my old friend.

Charles arrived and after the usual pleasantries and opening chat, enquired as to whether we would be off to church soon and received affirmation. His manner was somewhat reserved which added to my own reticence to start conversation. We were glad to see each other however our awkwardness was due to the circumstances of our separate departures from Africa. He had a tale to tell, but knew nothing of my circumstances and I none at all about him. He did look worse for wear which was upsetting. Charles was never blessed with an abundance of surplus body fat, but I must have appeared a sorry specimen to him, having lost two stone in weight, apart from other bodily characteristics, for he 'kindly' brought these to my attention.

Naturally I had to give some explanation and to a certain degree the flood gates of my feelings were opened. I informed Charles how I had to leave Africa very suddenly and thereby leaving behind my friends, the boys in the mission, my job and my goods and seven cats. I had arrived in Britain with an overwhelming sense of failure in my work for The Lord, had been treated as an unusual object of sympathy by some of my old church friends (and correctly by others) but with it seemed with disbelief when asked to give witness to my departure. The result was a de-motivation leading to a state of near depression. We both agreed after many years in Africa settling back into a comfortable environment proves difficult in itself, without having to bear burdens. In my case all the values I held in Africa simply did not apply to life in a sleepy Suffolk village. I also explained that I did not have prospects of employment and despite the generosity of my former employers my resources were rapidly dwindling. This seemed to make Charles even more subdued and I felt that instead of encouraging my friend, I was burdening him further. However, as a V.S.O he had security of tenure for his employment, but I did not.

So in a state of sombre empathy we did wend our way to church.

The communion was not spectacular, but for me ever since my baptism of fire I have never had anything but a rewarding personal communication with my Maker, when in the company of similarly minded people who are determined to praise and worship their God. It has always been like this and I know it always will be, no matter what my personal situation in this world. I know that I am in the Kingdom and I know the saints. Charles on the other hand appeared increasingly disturbed as the service developed. His behaviour was one of acute agitation. On enquiry he told me that he thought he had a word for the church but because he had never had one of these before he lacked the courage to get up and say something. I was surprised, out of my depth to help, and frustrated on his behalf but mumbled that he should do it. Because of my own disbelief that God would talk to a comfortable Baptist Chapel, and that that no 'word' similar to this had ever been given to me, I think my exhortation lacked conviction. The word was never delivered and poor Charles was so distraught I had to physically restrain him from leaving the building early and forced him to stay till the end. I do remember we hurriedly left the place and I remember sitting in my car doing my utmost to console him. I said that if he still wanted to deliver the message to the minister of the church we could still do this but he declined the offer. I then asked him if he wanted to impart it to me so that I might pass it on at a later stage, but only if that was what God wanted. It was evident that matters would not improve so I persuaded him to unburden himself. To the best of my memory he said, "Let go...the job is done...go on to pastures new."

It was a good few seconds before I realised that The Lord had sent a messenger to me and not the church. It was a further good few seconds for Charles to understand my ecstatic joy. Not only had my God chosen to give me a sign but had chosen for it to be delivered by a friend from Africa, in the most unusual way. Hallelujah!

After Charles's departure my life took on a new meaning. Much to the relief of my family and closest friends, I was able to off-load all the guilt I had felt on leaving my ministry. I put on weight and could actually laugh and entered back into church life without being treated as some form of leper. I could happily talk about

Africa and all its implications on my life and probably went overboard in my enthusiasm to relate as to what it was like to be at the sharp end. I have not lost that enthusiasm, but I think it is significant to note that no leadership of any church, that I have been a member of since leaving Africa, has ever asked to me to expound on my experiences. I believe there are three possibilities for this. The first concerns the fact that I went out to Africa without the backing of a recognisable church body. I realised the enormity of this 'failure' after subsequent conversations with clergy. As soon as this error was exposed, polite excuses were made terminate any need for a witness. On checking scripture I found that Paul suffered the same problem so at least there was an ancient precedent which put me at ease. The second was due to the fact that I was, and still am, sometimes overpowering in my zeal for Christ, my rhetoric can be a bit heady with excitement. I know that I am often loved or loathed, believed or un-believed, but somewhere in the middle of my idiosyncrasies is a good message for people that drives me on and gets the work done. Criticism does not worry me or deter me for a moment, for when in my weaker moments I ask The Lord if I am still acceptable to him in my pathetic ministry, he always brings confirmation and encouragement. The third reason is simple in that God did not want the full story told until now and so I will begin to unfold it in the pages of this book.

In Suffolk there was simply no use brooding further over anything, particularly as my sojourn in in another continent was over and I had to apply myself to the tasks and problems in hand. However I did not consider this daunting, for the solution to our future was obvious. As I had been a *super-missionary* who had been forcibly led back into Britain, I should become a cleric, a pastor or a priest. Which particular bent what not a consideration for I was broadminded enough to spend considerable time explaining to people that all denominations were an anathema to true Christianity and the teachings of Jesus, so I would graciously enter into any college where there was a suitable empathy towards my own cause. The fact that this was arrogant as well as detrimental to any future employment seemed to escape me, in my zeal. In any case I was convinced that God would choose for me and of course He did.

My only problem was that, having believed that I was actually a 'super-Christian' and having been spoken to by The Lord I had made one large miscalculation. God did not want me to become a cleric, pastor or priest and the ultimate realisation of this when it finally occurred was a considerable blow to my self-righteousness and future. Nevertheless the knowledge was not with me at that time and so I ploughed on.

Having been a lay reader in the Anglican diocese in Africa, this was my first port of call in the U.K. and everything went exceedingly smoothly until it became clear that I had suffered an unregenerate divorce many years previously. Surely this did not apply to me? After all I was a qualified Anglican lay reader, who has pastored a church for a year! Everyone was very considerate and I was assured that it was only a matter of time before the Church changed its mind, however a certain Mr Gummer was quite vociferous in the Synod about 'tainted' applicants and when I studied his communications on the subject I began to believe he had it in for me personally. My entreaties to any hierarchy pointing out that I had divorced when unregenerate, was now born again, and therefore forgiven by Jesus, fell largely on very nice but deaf ears. Jesus may well forgive the sin but sadly the Church of England could not, even after I had pleaded that time was running out for ordination as I was approaching the age barrier, precluding my entry into college leading to employment in stipendiary posts. I reminded people that God had a different set of rules when he came to bestow ministries on great men in the Bible, but it was pointed out that at least they were great!

My next port of call was the United Reform church of which I had attended on and off. This was also a 'cast iron certainty' as the minister of the church in our village was a personal friend and a lovely man. He knew about my 'baptism of fire' and considered that I would make an excellent minister and the denomination did not worry about unregenerate divorces. He would speak on my behalf and so the time arrived for my interview with the District Superintendent. I am not going to say too much about this event except that I have had to perform penance over my thoughts about the gentleman. This man found me to be very weak in my acceptance of doctrines of various religions especially disliking my argument that I hoped I would embrace that of the denomination which would give me the break I needed. It seemed more important to be grounded in the belief of one's church ideology and be willing to die for that, before God, or so it seemed to me. The news of my rejection however was taken very badly by my friend David Deans, who had personally recommended me. He suffered far more than I did which was both surprising and comforting. He is now in Head Office and I cannot wait for the day to come for me to explain to him about all the intricacies of my subsequent ministry. I heaven we will probably have a good laugh together.

The final attempt, which by now was so feeble that I should never have bothered, was to enter the ministry of the Baptist Church. Again this was via people who knew me personally, but here I did not get past the starting post. I think I spent the opening exchanges persuading those who were talking to me that I was in fact a journeyman and should be ignored as my doctrines were weak along with my faith and strength. I had become so demoralised over the fact that that 'The Church' seemed so absurdly silly in failing to recognize what was being offered under its nose that I virtually gave up during the interview and apologised for taking up their time. They smiled as I departed quietly.

My wife was the one to hit me between the eyes with the suggestion that it was highly probable that God did not want me to be a minister, within the Church per se, but felt that through the aforementioned interviews God must have been teaching me more about myself. This of course upset me considerably and after which I wasted much time and effort, proving she was right. Since then this lady has had three words of knowledge for me which were life changing. One example was that she once stopped a church service by informing me that The Lord insisted

I give up smoking my pipe. As I had asked The Lord two days before whether I should do such a thing, while on business 60 miles from the bosom of my family and without informing them of my request, I was overjoyed, much to the dismay of the preacher who wished to carry on with his message. He did so and I was able to give up 'cold turkey' with not so much of reaction after 38 years of smoking the briar.

Such is the power of The Lord when were both faithful to his commands. So it was with this gift that my wife told me I was not to pursue a ministry as a cleric. Since that day however I have been a Sunday school teacher, Mission Secretary, Youth Worker and Prayer Group Leader (which was the one ministry that gave me most satisfaction) and has culminated in hosting a House Church.

Outside the Church, the gifts and ministries acquired in Africa, much to my surprise, have continued although on a much reduced scale. This is probably due to the fact that I am into deliverance, spiritual warfare, healing and discipleship. Very few recognise such ministries, let alone avail themselves. These ministries not only do not fit into many a church curriculum and in some cases are considered taboo within their new age gospel. Some even believe that God being a woman, can never be never angry or vengeful, and not only has promised to keep us safe but all will go to tiered positions in heaven, even the most wicked. There is no hell, nor repentance needed, but just love and more love needed. If there is anyone reading this who cannot actually distinguish between what I have just written and the true Gospel, then please throw this book away. To continue to read it would mean that a true understanding of the power of the Gospel of Christ would change a life forever.

So, after more soul searching, I remained in England without a ministry, job and money. The Department of Health and Social security decided, after weeks of deliberation, I was entitled to around £37 a week to keep the family alive. This was fair as I had chosen to desert these shores for many a year and had not paid for a full insurance stamp while I had been away. My out-goings per week mostly due to a mortgage on my house was around £200, so disaster was inevitable. If it had not been for my former employers, good Christian friends, some of whom I know helped us and I therefore would not embarrass them by mentioning names, we would not have survived for so long. Money, at times fell, if not poured, through our letter box and so if anyone reading this was a contributor, then my wife and I thank you from the bottom of our hearts.

In order to survive I had to take a job. Not easy when passed the 45 barrier and your last reference showed work in a lab in Africa to raise a stipend to run a Christian mission, which finally created so much havoc it led to ejection from the country. I applied for 138 jobs before the Lord stepped in with one that suited my qualifications, experience and expertise to the tee, however before he did so I needed something short term and it came via a delightful gentleman who sidled up to me one day in church. The conversation we had went something like this:-

"Hello you probably don't know me...well you would know my wife. She attends more than I do and well I hear you're looking for a job, what with you being out of Africa and all that."

"Yes I am thank you. Do you have one for me?"

"Yes I do. It's not well paid, and you probably will not like it what with you being a scientist and all that, and I do not know how long it would last but maybe you should visit our workshops and have a look. My wife thought....with all your troubles, you know...."

"I'll take it."

"But is it true you are a scientist?"

"Yes, I was a sort of one."

"Do you know anything about the furniture business?"

"No nothing, but I am sure I'd learn."

"Have you ever polished or stained furniture?"

"No."

"Have you ever restored furniture?"

"No."

"Did you do woodwork at school?"

"No just metal work, but I once made a bed out of the Readers Digest Do-it-Yourself- Manual."

"I don't think you will like this job."

"When can I start?"

"We'll give you a week, to see how you go."

"I'll be there at 7 o'clock tomorrow."

The job lasted four months. It was one of the happiest times of my life. I learned how to stain and polish pine furniture and even acquired the skills to make it look antiquated. I became good at it and I was paid less than £1 an hour, working throughout a winter in a barn that at the best of times was freezing. Throughout the period I constantly read the Bible and got to know Job personally. I really knew him. I also found that I was a witness to my boss, for although a church goer was actually a non-believer! I informed him the good Lord would eventually provide me with a job within my profession which He did, and I parted company with this couple and their business on amicable terms.

Owing to our diminishing fortunes and despite the money received from the DHSS, Christians and my employers, our house and car came within a couple of days of repossession. At times we lived on bread and butter and some covering like jam while at other times we had a little more and through all this my wife was suffering a chronic liver and kidney complaint and I was to be struck down by a mystery illness. The root of these illnesses was to be found in Africa and even though I am the first to be plunged into any situation requiring healing, it must be clear to everyone that The Lord heals in His way and in His time. What he has promised us is sufficient grace to go through a day and we have gloriously claimed that in our family on many an occasion.

My wife was stricken by a virus in Africa and this was so debilitating that she had to be flown home and stayed on to receive treatment, much to my disappointment. It was not life threatening but she needed to be hospitalised occasionally and it was the right course of action in view of what was to occur. I thought I had escaped 'the bug' as I was very fit in Africa taking every available opportunity to play tennis and swim in the pounding surf in the sea. Not a bit of it. A year later I developed a 'frozen shoulder.' This had become evident during my furniture job and a few weeks later my other shoulder was smitten, so I was without the use of both of my arms. I could not dress myself without help.

Whatever ever the medical profession may say, for whom I occasionally have the highest regard, this was a latent virus creating some auto-immune 'blow up' that resulted in a serious condition. A hurried appointment was arranged at a hospital miles away and I saw a consultant, who after a very painful examination informed me that the prognosis was not good. It was unusual, though not unheard of, to have both shoulders frozen at the same time, but it was the extent of both the condition and the lack of flexion in my arms that worried him. The only treatment was steroid injections, as nasty as they sounded for they had to be given right into to the joint capsule. I was further unimpressed at the success rate when told if 'lucky' I could get back between 25- 50% rotation in my 'bad arm.' I was convinced this was a diabolical attack but went along to another hospital, also miles away for treatment. I also suffered a severe dose of PLM (poor little me, syndrome) at the time.

I know others who have had the treatment and have suffered only slight discomfort but I never want to go through it again. This however was unimportant when compared with how The Lord had arranged my healing through a lady consultant. I had opted to have both shoulders to be done at the same time and this lady, although concerned, did agree to carry out the procedure. She confirmed the low success rate and possible prognosis for my condition and while talking to me noticed the little cross of Jesus in my lapel.

"Do you believe you can be healed by God?"

"Yes," I replied. "Are you a believer sister?"

She was and we decided through my pain we would pray together. This was also her last medical act before retirement. So through tears we parted company. I had been informed that I would go through two days of agony, which I did, not even knowing or caring where I was, after which the pain would diminish fairly rapidly, which it did. These days included Christmas and Boxing Day. There would be a slow return to whatever restoration was permitted me. Within one week I had obtained over 60% rotation and today I am completely healed in one arm with 90% rotation in the other. It was the end of any racquet game that I particularly enjoyed. The Lord does remind me of his grace from time to time when I get twinges in wet weather and other climatic conditions, but I often wonder what would have occurred if The Lord had not sent this lady across my path, to literally give me a helping hand. I hope this dear lady's retirement has been blessed beyond imagination and of course I often think of her. I did contact her to tell her about my miraculous healing and remember both her joy and sadness for all those wasted years when she could have used the gift in healing. She was wrong to feel so sad, but there was nothing I could do or say to comfort her. I heard later that she was serving as a missionary doctor in Africa. So much for retirement! His wonders are constant to behold.

Suitably healed and patched up, my wife and I looked forward to a new life in Buckinghamshire where I was once again to enter the business world in my chosen profession, as a biomedical export manager for a pharmaceutical company. Africa was far behind me and there were wonderful ministries ahead as well as further times of hardship and struggle, however permit me now to go back to where it all began in that same sleepy old village in Suffolk, some six years previously.

Chapter 2: The Call

Some fifteen years prior to the writing of this book, if someone had asked me did I believe in God, I would have said it was possible that he could exist. Any further enquiries as to my spiritual state would have made the questioner realise that it was important for me to fit God, if he existed, into my life and at my convenience. If He did not interfere with what I wanted to achieve that would be fine. I did not attend any church but the problem with my life was that he continually appeared to interfere and it really annoyed me. He made sure that I would somehow, as a devil's advocate, and plead his existence in some seedy bar corner in Germany or He would jog my conscience when a colleague of mine kicked a beggar out of the way in Lahore or made me feel so guilty that I had to shy away from the dubious delights of the Snake Market in Taipei. Why couldn't I be like my peers? He messed up my life continually with his conscience probing. I could never quite get drunk, nor quite walk through that red door, nor quite agree on a shady deal that would bring me some commission I did not deserve. It was awful. Worse still I could not quite stretch my expenses as others did to include little presents for their wives or girlfriends or both! My peers disliked me intensely for this, especially my bosses as it spotlighted their own selfish and dishonest ways. Yes, He sure messed up my life and the enraging part about it was that I did not know why I behaved in this way.

I have spent many a lonely and agonising walk in some Godforsaken town in distant countries trying to fathom out why I was such a coward and jeered at by my colleagues.

After jobs based in Kuwait, Jordan and Singapore, I had ended up back in Suffolk which was my base for a new role as a freelance consultant. Working for agencies, I would advise people on various global biomedical markets or how much it would cost them to set up a laboratory or institution in a far flung post of the Empire. The job was well paid and involved travel and the gathering of a great deal of information. This was then for sale, especially for use in market surveys. After a year of this I was yet again looking for something that would bring real fulfilment and I finally considered a dream or vision that both my wife and I had years previously.

I am still not clear as to whether this is somehow born out of some desire of the two of us, or whether it was from The Lord, or merely whim, but independently we both had dreams that one day we would be running an establishment, whereby we would be looking after people who appeared to be enjoying themselves. At times on recollection this has resembled a bed and breakfast or guest house and at others a full scale Conference Centre. This may appear strange to the reader but strange things did happen to us. However fifteen years ago I decided that this must mean we were to run a hotel and so set about drawing up business plans to acquire various establishments. In succession, we would make a series of visits to these places, satisfy ourselves that we would want the hotel, carry on throughout the negotiation with all the requisite parties to include bankers and solicitors only to have the prize snatched away from us at the last moment. The reasons would be varied from 'gazumping' to a simple change of mind. It was one of the most frustrating periods of my life and unbeknown to me my wife and mother, both Christians, were praying for my salvation and asking The Lord to put stumbling blocks in front of each scheme. They felt I was merely going ahead to comply with some self-gratification. However at this time I tried to analyse my life in a useless effort to determine what was wrong. I was an itinerant consultant with bags of experience but was thoroughly frustrated at every turn. There was no answer and because of my failures my dream to acquire a hotel became obsessive. It became a battle I was determined to win. Every time I failed to get hold of an establishment the determination grew. I think I must have dragged my little family around half the hotels for sale at that time in East Anglia, Lincolnshire and Northamptonshire but I could not see their reticence, and even if I did I would have chosen to ignore it.

I was getting angrier and angrier and disgruntled with my wife. I hardly had any interest in my older two children John and Amanda and my mother was beginning to be a 'pain in the neck.' It is a total mystery how anyone can be so blind to the obvious when it stares them in the face. I remember even telling God how useless he was to me when I needed him to give me a hotel. Now, I am really ashamed yet so humbled under his love for me. I became a very angry, bitter, disillusioned, middle aged business man getting nowhere and spending a lot of time down at the local hostelries trying to work out what it was I needed to advance my ambition which was to become very rich at the expense of others. I toyed with the idea of the Parish Council, nearly got into the local wine club and brewery, flirted with Rotary and even considered the local lodge as the answer. They were wooing me for membership with lots of promises.

I was in a mess and I knew it and I also knew that something had to be done otherwise I was going to end up on some sort of scrap heap of life. I would fool myself into believing the sacrifice of my marriage and family was all part of the natural process of making a man rich. After all it happened to the male acquaintances around me. They were well off, worked like mad to earn money, kept a good accountant to ensure they paid virtually no tax, had holidays abroad and the occasional dalliance, if not actually supporting a mistress. To my credit, or should I say the grace of God, I considered that this could not be the right way to live and eventually decided that I wanted no part of it. But then, if this had to go what was left in the world for me apart from an enormous vacuum?

I remember the day well. It was beautiful weather at the end of May and I was miserable. I could not work on my present consultancy project. My previous one worth thousands of pounds had been lost by The Post Office despite arrangements for a special delivery to meet a deadline, culminating in me losing the faith of an agency and a lot of money. As I had not the heart to type up the notes once again so I sold the publishing rights to the agency, at a considerable loss. I felt so lonely and desperate that I had to get out of my office and into fresh air. I remember that this did not help much and seriously wondered if I was actually losing my mind. I did not want to greet people on this walk for in my paranoid state everyone appeared to be so happy with their lives. I stumbled on down the old high street of Clare until I came face to face with the Baptist Chapel. Remembering that it was open that day for meditation and prayer, I went in. The church to my recollection was empty and after seating myself I found that I started talking to this imaginary God. I railed, blaming Him for the failure of my life. After all had I not been in the choir as a boy? Had I not been an Acolyte at the altar and attended mid-night mass for at least 10 years of my life? "Does this not count for anything?" I shouted. I ranted and raved and the rest is still a blur.

I do remember something inside me being drawn back like a flood gate and a whole torrent of my sins poured out on the floor of that chapel. I begged him to forgive me as I was rotten to the core. What was said after that point is either lost or withdrawn from memory but remember that suddenly I was struck by revelation as though I knew who Jesus was for the first time. I also knew about sin, repentance, salvation, baptism in the Holy Spirit, and never, never, turning back. This statement seems incredible but nevertheless it is true. I received this baptism in the Spirit in exactly the same way I imagine Paul received his. His grounding was in the Sanhedrin, and my grounding had been in Roman Catholicism and I am presuming all the references locked away in our respective minds were at a stroke made real and became alive. That is my only explanation for this phenomenon. Neither he nor I were ever the same again. That is why I have to record these humble events. That is why he took the Gospel to the world in his stupendous mission.

Importantly I knew I had been forgiven and restored. I knew that I had actually come home but physically gone nowhere. Virtually ignorant of deep scripture, I had little idea I had received grace equal to that poured out on a road to Damascus 2000 years previously.

What is clear is that I emerged into daylight thinking I had been in the church for around 20 minutes but finding that I had been in the building for two and a quarter hours. I was utterly amazed. A worried wife had been trying to contact me to find out why I had not been back for lunch and not in my office. Then I wondered if anyone came in or out of the church during that time I was there and witnessed the extraordinary confession in part or whole. I still find it difficult to believe there were no witnesses, yet in the ensuing years not one person has ever admitted to being present. If there had been temple steps available I think I would have launched into some sort of soliloquy, such was my reverie.

As it was I left the church feeling clean and light and joyous. All the feelings that I experienced on that day I know will be shared by many a reader when they were born again; the same as Bunyan's pilgrim. The boulder had rolled off of my back and although I did not completely understand it, Jesus had already accepted and paid for that particular burden. Importantly I felt clear headed and purposeful as though a secret tryst had been made, and I half walked, half ran, back to my office, accosting people on the way, telling them that Jesus lives! For the first time in my life he was not just he was not a dead saviour on a cross.

There now followed a succession of miracles which, when put in context with what is described later in the book, are not so dramatic but nevertheless gave me a foretaste of what was to come. Please remember at this time I am only barely aware I have been born again let alone being blessed, so it would be a surprise to note all that happened caused me fright as well as amazement.

I entered my locked office to find that the gazette to my professional Institute had been delivered, and was on the floor. I picked up and put on my desk. I was still in a state of euphoria but after a while realised the significance of the magazine being in my room. It had not been there before I left, but it was there when I entered through door I unlocked. In checking with the staff of the two other companies that shared the building, nobody recalled having delivered the magazine to my office. I suppose someone could have shoved it under the door. Ignoring this for the moment I remember sitting at my desk and trying to work out what I tell my family concerning my experience, What was my experience?, How do I apologise to my family? I remember a telephone conversation with my wife telling her that I was alright but had changed and would explain later. Only after this call did I begin to understand there was a divine intervention in the matter of my gazette. After opening the packet I turned the pages slowly and was almost through when I came to an advertisement near the back for a Chief Technician required by a British premier Medical Unit in Africa. This was a quasi-civil service post and one I had no chance of getting.

I was over-aged sales and marketing executive without the complete set of qualifications needed and a little record of any practical experience at the bench in years. Anyway why was I interested at all in this position? Africa was the last place that I wanted to go to and yet even at that moment there was an infectious desire to apply.

When I tried to dismiss this advert and turn over the page in the gazette I found that I had no strength to do so. I remember feeling out of control and memory has dimmed as to exactly what happened throughout that afternoon but what I do know is that I had my application with a C.V. sealed in an envelope in good time to catch the last post that day. It was as though I had watched another person applying for this crazy position.

It is also difficult to describe how I felt when I went home, as though I was entering it and talking to my family, for the first time. It was equally difficult to explain that I had been 'born again' for I hardly realised it myself. I was not even aware of such a thing in my grounding. I was confirmed by a Bishop with ashes spread on my forehead but nothing happened to me at all. I remember be very disillusioned at the time. However, no trumpet blared outside number 45 and in truth everyone was a little suspicious of me but as time went by it was obvious that I was changing in my attitude to family, people, church and life in general however. Satan, however, had one very nasty last trick up his sleeve to try and persuade me to go down a road to perdition. I now know he was allowed to test me, while my sweet Lord waited in the wings.

One last die had been cast to secure a hotel. A local public house with guest rooms had come onto the market. I had previously negotiated for it and had persuaded my wife that this was the place for us. We had worked out how we could also keep our house in the village and how we could work in shifts, interacting occasionally with the children and meeting up all together, maybe 2 or 3 times a year! My wife and mother were worried but I re-assured them that this was the start of our bid for wealth. Very soon we would be making so much money that I would appoint a manager and things would be a lot better for all of us. In truth they were both horrified as well as being mystified. Once again they went into prayer to protect me from such folly but a few days after my deliverance came the terrific news the place was ours for the asking.

The owners had accepted a much reduced offer and the bank was very happy at the new deal. My solicitor and advisors were saying that I should sign without delay. Initially, I admit to being overjoyed and the solicitor brought over the requisite papers in the evening and I was told to have them ready for the morrow, when they would be an exchange of contracts. I even poured myself a celebration drink and sat gloating over the papers. It was mine for the taking at last. The dream was coming true or was it? The more I stared the more I felt unease and the innumerable reasons for rejecting such a project started to fill my mind. I have never feared anything but the uselessness of this pursuit dawned on me and I began to be petrified at what I was being led into. What on earth was I about to do? Seeing reason I walked up to my frantic wife and told her I would not be taking the place. I don't think I have seen her so overjoyed before or since but this led me with one of the most distressing moments of my life. I had to go and tell the owners of the pub with whom I had struck such a hard bargain. I can remember the conversation as though it were yesterday. I arrived to find the couple in the bar giving the place a good clean in anticipation of a visit.

"Well now!" said the landlord. "Congratulations, I don't suppose you can believe it?"

He went to explain that because of their personal circumstances they had decided to move out quicker than expected. Even though my offer was ridiculous, I was the only applicant who could complete in time to suit their needs.

"So the place is yours. We would like you and your wife to carry on in the tradition of this old place; as you are resident in the village."

I can remember exactly what I said in reply.

"I'm sorry but I cannot take over this pub. I have just become a Christian and my God has told me that there are other plans for me. I hope it is understood that something happened to me that cannot be changed. I'm very sorry for your disappointment."

A stunned silence was followed by a certain amount of verbal disbelief, which both confused and frightened me. In my new euphoric spiritual state I actually had expected them to understand because God was in charge. Where was He? I just sat in that lounge bar throughout the tirade and kept telling myself that it would be all right. It would work out because God understands so "will you please stop shouting at me." I was colourfully informed that I must be some kind of peculiar Christian to go back on my word after giving them so much hope. I almost faltered at this hurdle until I realised I had not completed a contract, but merely an offer and although I had bargained considerably I was not actually reneging on anything, as my signature had not been penned. The abuse continued as they begged me to reconsider. It was awful.

Eventually the heat came out of the one way conversation and everything reverted to a silent atmosphere of despair, which made me feel worse and so after a while I got up to go. I then decided to take my very first leap of faith. I informed them that it was not right that I should let them down in this way and in view of their circumstances they should be able to sell up and move away. They were informed I would ask The Lord to bring a new client who would be wishing to close a deal with them in the shortest possible time. This enraged them but, thank God I was merely asked to leave, which I did, however the final irony in this story is that this couple completed a deal two weeks later with a surprise buyer at a price of £15,000 more than my offer. What is more, the reason for them to move away evaporated and they stayed on in the village for a few months before purchasing a larger hotel somewhere else. My friendship improved from the broken position I had left them in. They eventually considered, although I was a rat, I had done them a good turn. One up for The Lord! Once again I felt clean. I had done what The Lord required of me, or so I thought. I had given up my dream and starting to consider that every aspect of my life should be handed over to His discernment. The first thing God did was to lay a desire on my heart to 'devour' The Bible.

I came under the occasional ministry of my friend David Deans and learned that no matter what knowledge was acquired by a man and no matter what giddy heights he might raise himself to in service to God nothing substituted for a loving character, a willingness to serve and a heart for mankind. Dear David taught me about practical Christianity first and encouraged me to realise if I managed to get that right then all the theological stuff would follow in due course. How right he was and I can thoroughly recommend this approach to discipleship. Under The

Holy Spirit's tutelage through David, His ever faithful servant, I sought and found the Kingdom and waited for the other things to be added. (Matthew 6:32)

Added they were and followed thick and fast. Members of the family started to like each other and we even prayed together. Church was exciting and as though new for the first time. Sermons started to have meaning. Warmth and love started to creep into our lives. There was however one problem in my life, when all else appeared to be rosy. The job in Africa I had applied on a supposed whim of fancy became a reality and I had been accepted for the first round of interviews. Even then, each time I had any successful news concerning my progress in the application I would brush it off as silliness. I convinced myself there was no possible chance in getting this position as I had no intention of going to Africa and there was also no chance for me in competition with others. I decided that it was a useful exercise to experience, particularly as my own resources had diminished alarmingly and I was looking for work. Naturally I had not told my family about this application but being incommunicado over this subject was starting to disturb me.

At the final interview I actually argued against myself in the same fashion as I did at Baptist interview. I heard there was an internal candidate, which proved to me that I had no chance, however all my self-effacing was fruitless as the Institute was apparently looking for just such a chap as me, who had good business sense coupled with a laboratory background. Apparently I had the character needed to clear up a little mess that had developed within the logistics of the centre. The little logistic problem turned out to be a very big financial and logistical mess, but after arriving and discovering the truth I actually relished the opportunity to put matters right.

Finally, I was asked to give a date when I could arrive at my post. I replied I would be in post within two months. We shook hands all round and I left the building in a daze. I remember standing outside the portals of this old seat of tropical learning wondering how I could tell my wife, let alone family, that I was off to Africa.

Chapter 3: Africa

Before we set foot in Africa I want to say I make no excuses for this chapter being so long, for I aim to give a correct 'flavour' of what it is like to live and work in an unusual environment, that is for both a white man and a Christian, especially if there is a desire to suffer apparent hardships as missionary. Of course, the same kind of conditions could be met with wherever anyone settled but it is important to know what should be mentally addressed before leaving on such an adventure. On balance there are always so many good things that can happen in a strange environment that they far outweigh any deprivation; others sadly may not agree but it is an attitude of mind that brings rewards. If there is the slightest trepidation, either bad things will happen or even normal events will seem like a nightmare. The right approach to everything will bring these rewards instead of sacrifices but if fear and dread outweighs any longing then my advice would be to never leave home. When I set off anywhere in the world it always will be with excited anticipation. Even at this time, having travelled now in over eighty countries there is always the thrill of arriving somewhere new.

I knew not to be lulled into the false sense of security that the comfortable British Caledonian aircraft was affording me on the way out to a new life. As I peered out of the window, there appeared a country largely inhospitable that would be full of unwanted surprises. However this time I was arriving in a country to which God had assigned me and that made all the difference and armed with my Bible and carrying my duty free items, I entered the environment of sub-tropical Africa for the first time.

Sure enough, I was plunged into a temperature at least 20 degrees warmer than the country I had left, even though it was the start of the cool season, and the dust swirled up to brush my face, which was already contorted to keep the searing sun from abusing my eyeballs. I was here on a mission and only God knew what that was supposed to be, so taking a deep breath I climbed down the steps of the aircraft and set off across the tarmac for the short walk to the terminal building.

There was an unexpected scrum at the custom's trestle tables as we poured over a pile of luggage in order to select our own and soon I was thrust outside the perimeter fence, feeling that I had really arrived. After dumping my luggage and locating my driver next to a slightly battered Land Rover that bore the name of the research unit, we set off at a reasonable pace towards the bush. I marvelled at the metalling of the road. Superb by any standards, it had nicely painted curb stones in places and the whole was lined by trees, but I soon realised that this was unfortunately for show only. After half a mile we came to a T junction where we turned right onto a normal main road which, like the curate's egg, was good in parts. Where it was bad it was very, very bad, with deep potholes inviting any vehicular suspension to take them on. We did our best and I was now very grateful to be in Land Rover, battered or not. I also soon realised that the vehicle I was travelling in was in pristine condition compared to others as we bumped the 20 odd miles or so to my residence. This turned out to be an old corroding metal and white asbestos building, which was once the pilot's mess of the Lufthansa Airline Company, when flying boats actually touched down in the bay. How romantic! I had one room with toilet/bathroom down the corridor. I was given a huge metal key to my door and before I knew it, I was on my own. The smell of mildew pervaded and while I battled with the one air-conditioning unit, I realised I was sweating profusely. This was a condition I would have to get used to if I wanted to stay in Africa as well as its secondary evil called prickly heat.

There was a letter addressed to me on the bed, informing me that the head of the laboratory would pick me up at an appointed time for dinner that evening, so I unpacked my dank clothes into a dank wardrobe, made an fairly unsuccessful attempt at a shower, poured myself a duty free drink, and lay half naked on my dank bed under the booming air conditioner and pondered as to the circumstances that had brought me here. Pondering when there has been a plunge into the unknown often occurs when it is too late to do anything about it. I was well and truly ensconced.

The blessed Holy Spirit.

I saw myself standing outside my house in Clare, Suffolk, wondering just how I was supposed to handle a really big problem. Not two hours previously I informed a row of well suited gentlemen that I would take up a technicians post in Africa, within two months from that day. I also informed them that I would be leaving my two eldest children in school in Britain and that they would live at my house, while my ageing mother would look after them. I also informed these gentlemen that after the requisite acclimatisation into my post, that my wife and youngest son would be joining me in Africa, for the duration. They were well pleased by my positive approach. The only thing I had to do now was tell my family.

As explained before, my major problem was that I had not told a single member that I was going, however I ask the reader not to make snap judgements concerning my apparent total lack of concern for the feelings of my dearest. My existence during the last few months had moved from the hard shoulder of life, not only into the fast lane but from a Morris Minor into a Ferrari. The moment I considered bearing all to my family, a new inexplicable event would occur to amaze and confuse me further. This caused impotency of mind as I battled with each new revelation. The emotional balloon grew alarmingly but it had to burst.

If I had told my family/friends that I had been born again, told by God to give up my job and apply for a post in Africa, all in one single afternoon, I would probably have been considered as a candidate for some heavy therapy. If I had told my wife that, despite her protestations that I had broken a promise to her concerning never working abroad again, but that God had engineered the whole process of me going to Africa and because I did not want to end up in the belly of a whale I would have to ignore her, therapy would have started. If I had told my children that I was possibly off to Africa, it would have realised doubts and concern, wondering whether they were to go or not, or indeed what the future would hold for their academic careers. If I had been able to inform everyone connected with me that in actual fact the job was only the means of a stipend for whatever The Lord had in mind as a ministry for me, but I had no idea what this was as yet, I would have been certified and carried away.

At the very least hostility from one or more quarters could have jeopardised the decision process where I might have given up travelling down the yellow brick road. If I had for one minute, faith as huge as a mustard seed and actually believed God was in control and stopped telling myself that the successive interviews for this crazy post was just a useful exercise and God did not really mean for me to go to Africa, then I would have probably handled everything better. But I was a thoroughly inexperienced convert who knew little about the power of God to shoulder these. So, it can be seen whatever course of action I might have considered taking, the cards appeared stacked against me. How often this appears to be the case when working for God? I was to face this time and again. So I hope if forgiveness is not metered out then there is at least an understanding of the dilemma I faced.

I stood by the hedge on the path that led up to the front door of number 45 Hertford Road. "Dear Holy Spirit. I know you exist but I know nothing about you. I believe that you are a fully-fledged member of the Trinity and already desperately need you to teach me before I start working in Africa. I also believe that you are a tremendous power and that if you want to, you can smooth everything out. Dear Lord I do not know what will happen right now but I am only doing what you told me to do, so it's not fair if it all goes wrong. I love my family deeply now but this could divide us for ever. Please help me." That was the gist of everything that I cried out to the Lord that day by the hedge. I took a deep breath and went into the house. I told my mother first who was overjoyed and was only too happy to look after the children. I told the children second and they became very excited and then somewhat subdued when they realised they would not be going. They were immediately mollified when I told them exciting holidays would be in the offing. Finally I told my wife. Last to be informed, but by no means least, she was upset that I had not told her in the first place. I explained that I had to make sure mum could cope with the children and that they could cope with us being away, otherwise there was no point to it all. Reluctantly she eventually understood but after taking her out a swanky hotel in the evening to bribe her further, it was she who was reaching for the few tourist brochures I had manage to acquire in London. These in my opinion were pretty pathetic and would not have attracted me set foot outside Suffolk, but she became very excited as the final act was played out in that lounge bar. He had triumphed and we were going! There was one other member of the family, dear Stephen aged four, who was consulted but as he thought that Africa was somewhere near Cambridge, I felt that we could get him out there without too much of a problem. I had not even approached a boarding school for the two eldest, but the one I chose only had two places left for a boy and a girl in the requisite dormitories for the requested time! This was further confirmation of God's wonderful power working in advance.

However, while lying on my bed back at the German mess, I had no idea what The Lord wanted me to do now that I was actually in the place. The following day was a Sunday and having got hold of a bicycle I rode up and down the streets of the nearest areas of habitation literally looking for churches. I decided that having arrived without any clear design, at least God would want to start with me becoming a member of a local church. Surely it would all start there? I decided I would enter into the one that 'felt right' after initial enquiries and if welcomed, I would join that fellowship. One cannot afford to be fussy when going abroad. If the traveller is High Church Anglican or Low United Reform, then life could be particularly difficult, however if there is an open mind about receiving whatever may happen could be pleasantly surprising. Having been warmly welcomed into a group called Southern Baptists from the U.S.A, and having an Anglican Mission Church virtually in the garden of the German mess, I decided to join both for a while.

I would attend the Anglican Sunday morning service and go to the Baptists in the late afternoon. My family when they came out would happily do the same. I had no idea at that time, that as a newly appointed Lay Reader and for one year, I would be the only 'priest' at that very same Anglican Mission Church. It is wonderful to know now, what God knew then.

Approximately six weeks after I had arrived in Africa, My wife and son joined me and we all moved into an old colonial style bungalow, with cavernous rooms, minimal furniture and a lovely veranda running around its entirety. The garden was nothing but a red dust bowl. One day an old Peugeot diesel front wheel drive shooting brake arrived at our door so we were well set for any family adventure into the bush. The labs were sound, the job was exciting and challenging and I was happy.

The Medical Complex

The laboratory I worked at from 7.30 a.m. till 3.00 p.m. each week day was situated in enormous grounds of 70 acres. During World War II it had been part of an army complex, incorporating an old military hospital and operating theatre. Apparently it was used as a recuperation base for the unfortunate wounded of various conflicts that took place in the continent. The church was the original army chapel of the hospital complex. Attached to all this was a brand new 50 bed hospital and a number of buildings which comprise the laboratory and stores. There were also a number of newer buildings, housing administrators, and service workshops, housing engineers and the like. The complex catered for the needs of a number of medical scientists, either employed or seconded from a number of universities in Britain, where they could come to grips with various tropical diseases.

They researched to further their particular programmes and academic careers. Medical students on placement also came and went. The laboratories were housed in four buildings to include the stores. The equipment was relatively up to date and computer driven. The stores however were not and I later sent samples of the earliest items I found, to a museum. These had entered Africa in 1955.

When I arrived the laboratory had one Ghanaian senior technician and about 15 other nationals who were at various stages of training and knowledge. One of my briefs was to arrange for an accredited course in technology and to ensure that these technicians could attain qualifications acceptable within Africa. With the help of another expatriate, a Dr Alan Smith who proved to be the local pathologist, this was achieved at some cost to our sanity.

I was asked to reorganise the labs and the stores, train the technicians both in laboratory diagnostics and in research work, reorganise and keep a tight rein on budgets, whether laboratory or those of the individual scientists and generally make things work when they would not. One major headache was to ensure all the logistics were in place for the scientists to carry out their research at five satellite laboratories, one of which was in an entirely different country. This would mean treks into the interior at regular intervals. It was at times real 'Indiana Jones' territory.

Each day the compound from about 6.30 a.m. onwards, was full of African patients. These underwent a sort of 'Quadrage' (triage, but with four stations). The gate keeper, one Demba, who was remarkably short on compassion and one of the most devious characters I ever met, was in charge of allowing only a set number of patients into the compound each day. He did this with precision. It did not matter a jot if anyone had walked 20 miles to get to the centre, if the allotted number for the day had passed through the gate, the remaining unfortunates had to come back the following day. Sometimes people actually camped outside to await the opening of the gates on the morrow. On more than one occasion I have had to half drag a dying patient inside while remonstrating with Demba and then had to explain my actions to the director of the laboratory, after he received complaints about my behaviour.

Demba disliked me intensely as I was a practising Christian and the more my fame or infamy spread abroad, the more he tried to deter me from my work, I have to say with some measurable success. Demba was the Imam of his own compound.

There are some things in life that can never change; the colour of skin; (Blood is thicker than water) grudging subservient behaviour; (Did not the British rule the world once?) a right to misappropriate. (The rich are there to be plundered) All this behaviour seems so alien to a disciple eager to serve, but very important to the life and existence of a native of the country. The ex-patriot had so much bitterness, so much bigotry, and so much righteous hatred to overcome, before he or she is able to be truly accepted, and only by the grace of God could success be achieved, by breaking the mould. Missionaries fare no better as there is the natural added suspicion of 'do-gooders' and charitable works often expose the pride of a person, which is often the only thing they have left to cling to. My director used to tell me that Demba did a wonderful job at the gate and had done so for twenty odd years. He often reminded me that we were living in someone else's country so who was I to complain? The fact that people were suffering and dying due to his own imposed rules did not seem to register with the gentleman. The fact that I dragged someone in who was dying was also irrelevant. "Africans die daily, it's the way of things. You'll see and you will change".

I never did.

Demba probably did perform a marvellous job and my Director was proud of the work his unit did, pointing out that I was too sensitive. "How many more would die if we were not here at all?" I may have been disproportionately sensitive, but I was glad that I was.

The hospital was relatively well equipped to make a difference in matters of life and death. However many were admitted with terminal conditions for which no hospital in the world could overcome. Malaria was the most common horror in the rainy season and one of the worst deaths to witness. It was especially hard to see the children dying. They lapsed into a semi-comatose state after which their eyes would roll and the body would be arched and racked with incessant panting which would increase to violent proportions until their little hearts gave out. All because there were simply not enough un-parasitized red cells in their blood stream, to carry sufficient oxygen around their bodies. They simply slowly suffocated and/or suffered heart failure. Malnutrition was easy to treat. Aids and sickle cell anaemia and an alarming number of liver cancer cases were also found on the ward. Every patient admitted simply filled up the next available bed. There was no discrimination between the sexes and no privacy, but what was that to the African?

If the native was ill and had fought their way into the compound via Demba, fought their way through the first outpatient screen, run by a local, they had to be seen by a European doctor at the clinic stage 3. Having been classified as sick enough for the hospital, which meant the person was in a bad way, transfer to the ward occurred. If there was a bed, and if the patient could afford the equivalent of £25 (by present day standards) admission followed. Otherwise, strange as though it may seem the applicant went home to try again; to go through the whole process the next day even if they were at death's door. Consequently, I along with others paid for many an admission during our tours.

There was a fleet of long wheel-base Land Rovers which transported us, our equipment and all the supplies around the country. The institution had its own petrol store, but this did not prevent us from having to go through shortages now and again. I ran a diesel vehicle and remember once being off the road for 3 weeks, awaiting a tanker to dock in the port.

We all lived in bungalows if we were married and in comfortable prefab flats if we were not. Most people ate a mixture of European and African dishes and employed a maid/cook and a gardener, for a pittance of a wage. We thought this demeaning until we realised it was giving employment, encouragement and witness to people and their families. We could not pay a decent wage as this would have caused havoc with the micro-economy of the place. We supplemented the wage in kind.

The local supermarket did its best to attract us, however what was put on the shelf were rejects and damaged goods purchased through agents who acquired all the unused stock from British Supermarket chain stores. What is not fit for Britain is good enough for this part of Africa. I remember once that it was reported that Cornflakes had hit town and sure enough in rushing to the market I found a few dented packets left on the shelf. Despite filtering out most of the weevils, I still ate the stuff with reasonable gusto, much to the disgust of my wife. Such was my deprivation which even as I write is a little hard to understand but I always did persevere.

If local meat was desired it was best to ask the butcher to shoo away the carpet of flies on the cut in order to determine its origin. However there was one butcher who boasted of imported meat. To his credit he did have N.Z. lamb and European cuts in his freezers, but they could only operate when electricity was supplied to them. As the national supply was often cut off for 12 hours or more at a time, it can only be imagined the sorry state of the freezer contents, especially in the summer months. They simply refroze when the power was put back on. I would sooner eat the meat from the local farm and lived by two principals. The first was that if there is belief in God's protection we can inadvertently take poison and it will never affect us, and secondly, being a medical man, no matter what was on or in the joint if it was cooked to perfection, nothing would happen to harm the body. Supporting scripture for this is found right at the end of the book of Mark.

Besides the occasional meat, the country abounded with fruits of the sea of which our favourite was butterfish but we also particularly liked a local fish-ball stew incorporating peanut gravy. We ate an awful lot of rice, which did not worry me having been born and brought up in Bangalore during my early years. The vegetable markets were a treat. All sorts of fascinating items abounded from varieties of peppers to sweet potatoes to local spinach and herbs. Ordinary potatoes did not grow to well which was disappointing. We had a sound diet practically free of fats.

There was no T.V. or radio, unless there was the ability to tune into BBC overseas service when the wind was in the right direction, however if there was a liking of the simple things such as an outdoor life, slowness of pace, easy going people, no pollution, little traffic and good healthy diet then Africa is the place, however there were a few who could not stand losing their creature comforts. For them, boiling water before consumption was too tedious a process. Unfortunately they could not balance the slight discomforts against the wealth of experiences and delights that Africa offered the adventurer. They usually left within weeks. Missionaries often had to put up with even greater hardships but found a rewarding life by being in the right place at the right time. Those who were not, suffered terribly.

The weather

The climate had distinct seasons just like back home in Britain, although autumn was a little difficult to determine. The seasons were always dominated by extreme heat, humidity or torrential rain, but there were some very pleasant months. A winter day may actually drop down to around 20°C and yet the locals would build fires wherever they could, around which they would huddle for warmth and drink tea. Nights did get down to about 15 degrees. An amusing sight in winter was to look for and note the differing fashions in knitted bobble caps and various other forms of headgear; very colourful and very practical.

For a third of the year there was always present a dry heat that slowly built up to around 30-35°C just prior to the rainy season. Then the humidity kicked in and the two months preceding the rains would be almost unbearable. It would rise to a proportion where everything would either be permanently wet or simply rot away. Clothes fell to pieces along with tempers. Nights were difficult to sleep through, unless the air-conditioning unit on was switched on. If this was done it was the equivalent of running an air compressor permanently two metres from the bed which would cut in and out at will; that is if there was any power at all. Another factor which precluded the use of A/C in our house was the expense, so we opted for lying under a slowly circulating ceiling fan while maintaining our modesty with the covering of a thin sheet. It worked when we got used to it.

Another diabolical curse is prickly heat which struck without warning and would rapidly spread across parts of the anatomy, often in very uncomfortable places. It would drive a person quite crazy at times with the continual hot itching. Fortunately for me the Laboratories were equipped with air conditioning which made life bearable during these months.

However the most spectacular effect on the weather was the Hammatan. When the rain came it was an enormous relief and people would stand and be soaked to the skin in seconds to pay homage to its arrival. However they swiftly moved inside as the storm's true ferocity broke loose. The Hammatan wind, like the Monsoon, which everyone has heard about, arrives to drop its rain on the red dust of central Africa. For weeks prior to this event there will be a huge build-up of cloud and people will say that it would definitely rain that day but it never did, until with delight it is confirmed to be raining 'up country'. Then the belief in rain brings excitement because the bush telegraph said so. A rain storm is always heralded by the wind. From a heavy stinking stillness, in which it is an effort to breathe, there is a sudden awareness that all the birds have disappeared. Then perceptible wisps of air appear that set the dust dancing around feet and the scraggy leaves in the trees are noted to be dancing in tune to a definite breeze which rapidly builds up to hurricane force. The sun vanishes as the lightning starts. The thunder reverberates all around as it begins to rain. Each drop seems the size of a small pebble and from a pitter-patter here and there, within seconds the downpour is so tremendous that there arises a fine spray from the force of the water hitting the ground. Within minutes the panorama changes as lakes appear which soon merge with each other and leave isolated islands, upon which there is the only hope for sanctuary if caught in the open. All the time the wind screams, thunder booms and the rain taps out an incessant machine gun rattle, especially on any tin roofs. It is breath-taking, awesome and frightening and is one of the most exciting events I have ever witnessed. As soon as it begins it may be over or it may choose to last for over an hour. I absolutely loved it and even in its full force would walk about revelling in its strength. There was a downside to these events which tested me on many an occasion. Imagine being out in one of these storms, when in the small hours of a morning I had to reconnect the electrical supply to the labs, via an emergency generator. It was an interesting exercise. I have never been so wet, nor experienced rain that hurt, until I went to Africa. Never have I had to pit my strength against such a storm anywhere else in the world, and that included residing in Singapore.

Also whipped up by the Hammatan, when it decides not to deposit rain, are storms of red choking dust. Everything turns an eerie red. The sun, the sky and anything that moves, remains in this perpetual twilight until mysteriously subsiding, but this could be days later.

The Flora and Fauna

Not much is left in the country after the ravages of the great white hunters and the incessant need of the native to cut down trees for use as firewood but when it rains a miracle occurs. Within minutes, or so it seems, growth springs into life. Seeds that lie dormant during two thirds of the arid yearly climate are activated and a profusion of small plants and grass arises from the ground. Most are insignificant, but one bush plant deserves special mention and that is the Bougainvillea. These flowering bushes are in utter profusion everywhere in the suburbs and the variety and colour is glorious to behold. One tree also deserves a mention, and after the rains its garlands of flowers, which resemble the lily family, are seen as a delight on its otherwise gnarled branches. The flowers exude a faint but delightful smell which is seductive in nature. The tree goes by the delightful name of the Frangipani and I believe its scent is used in the manufacture of commercial perfumes.

Of the fruits in the garden were found mango, papaya and nearby Jackfruit and above all, the most delicious grapefruit in the world. Each, in season, brought happy moments of eating. There were also plenty of groundnuts and cashews.

Where Elephant, lion, giraffe and ostrich roamed not so many years ago any hunter today is lucky if a baboon, jungle cat or bush pig is spied. The latter are the most dangerous of species to meet when travelling, notwithstanding the plethora of snakes which abound. I presumed most of the snakes that I came across on my nocturnal journeys were relatively harmless; I presumed? I found that all snakes were more frightened of me than I was of them, but the danger lay in accidentally treading on one that was sleeping.

Two of the most interesting animals were the bandicoot or African rat and the Monitor lizard. The former which grew up to the size of a large rabbit, was considered positively evil by one tribe and a delicious delicacy by another, so all in all I was very surprised that I saw the number I did. The latter character was fascinating, and although similarly hunted by the natives always seemed to be in large numbers on the compound. I found it a most beautiful creature that so resembled a dinosaur and its measured movements and flickering tongue were quite fascinating to watch, except when I was desperately trying to keep them away from my duck enclosure. I recall watching two of our cats on the one occasion they decided to attack a smaller version of the reptile. I feared for the monitor for this two pronged attack seemed certain to succeed, however I feared in vain. This slow moving creature moves very rapidly when it has to. Soon, by a flick of a powerful tail, one cat was flying throughout the air one way followed by the other cat the other way. The lizard then shot off at speed and I had to rescue two winded but otherwise apparently unharmed cats. I never again saw any one of the seven come close to launching an attack a Monitor Lizard.

There was a large variety of lizards everywhere but indoors was found the habitat of the delightful geckos. They gobbled up mosquitoes and the like and so were very useful but there was always a battle to keep the cats from them. The geckos were poisonous to the cats. Upon ingestion they had to immediately dispose of the meal, which was not too pleasant to witness. But nature being what it is they were always after the creatures.

One other animal I will mention and that was the chameleon. Again feared by the native, I was always fascinated by its ability to see in different directions at once, the variety and their colour changing ability and movements. I once watched a chameleon cross an up-station compound by jerking backwards and forwards on its little legs. It seemed to take two steps forwards and one back in every movement it made. I was determined to study it and the 10 yard journey from a building to a tree took over an hour. All sorts of things scurried up to it or swooped down upon it, but it was always left untouched. It knew what it was doing and I am sure its antics enabled it to survive the journey.

The Birds were beautiful with over three hundred separate species. I was well conversant with the art of photography and decided to take an image of all I came across. From the delightful Bee Eaters and Honey Suckers, which are like miniature humming birds, to the joy of seeing Pelicans, huge Cranes, Giant Hornbills and pretty Flamingos, all titillated. The smaller birds were all colours of the rainbow. I even developed a healthy respect for the varieties of buzzard and Vulture, which in my opinion are much maligned birds. To see an adult vulture of the largest species on the ground with its wings spread out to catch the sun, which is a cleaning process, is quite a sight. The one bird which gave me the greatest pleasure was the sea eagle.

We lived close to the ocean and in the evening just as the stifling heat of the day began to relent, the wind would blow in off the water to try and compensate the scorched land. It was my privilege and pleasure to walk up to the cliff overhangs, roughly 20 metres above the beach, and pray to The Lord to thank him for His creation. Whenever I was in Jafara I used to do this regularly, and every day when my family had left me to be in England. I was to be found at twilight at that particular spot, in rapture, singing away oblivious to everything around me except one. I knew I could not be here forever and I knew I had to drink in each moment for posterity. I always sang 'My Lord how great Thou art.' at the top of my voice. No-one ever disturbed me and the few travellers along the cliff path some 10 meters below merely smiled and waved at the crazy Englishman who was out singing again. However throughout this entire exercise my friends the eagles would come and simply hang in the wind, joyously riding the breeze until they would, with a screech of excitement, dive headlong down the cliff only to swoop up again and to re-suspend in mid-air. At first they stayed well away from me, but as we got to know each other they accepted my pacification and learned to honour my antics. It became a wonderful time of friendship. Can it be imagined what it is like to have an eagle just hanging in front, some 2-3 meters away as though on a string? And then there was another above and another below and soon everywhere around. There must have been thirty or so in the air at any given time. Only the slight movements of their wings and the ruffling of feathers betrayed the fact that they were in control. They appeared to like the sound of my voice. Occasionally they would fly close enough to be touched. I tried on occasions but they would gently move out of reach. They knew I wanted to do it but quietly chided me.

In the sea, it was nice to see dolphins play alongside ferry boats and in the river to see Herons above and hippos below, playing in the sweeter water.

The Insects

Most loathe them but I have a degree in Parasitology which means I must love them.

However, an immigrant could live in Africa and be both horrified and fascinated at the same time by whatever they came across.

I have always found ants the most industrious of God's creatures and in studying them we could all learn lessons about corporate behaviour. Termites however finally persuaded me to think differently about such insect types, although of course they are not ants. They were everywhere and although designed to scavenge the floor of God's earth in order to maintain equilibrium, they were no respecter of man's puny achievements to build in wood, or even concrete! An example of such voracity came home to me when the tree house I proudly built for my son in an eucalyptus tree next to our bungalow, was reduced to powder by the little 'so and so' in a matter of weeks. They even ate the ladder I used to get children up to the house. A termite hill in the bush can reach over 2 meters high and 1.5 in diameter, an amazing feat when its purpose for the nest far below is for air conditioning!

Spiders were sometimes massive and beetles abounded with their own special industries. There are three of which I especially wish to mention. The first appears literally after the first rains and lives for only a few days. They were conveniently known as 'rain bugs.' Everywhere one's eyes are glued to a scurrying mass of profusion of these little beetles covering the ground. They are half the size of a lady bird. On close examination they were covered with a fine sheen of a vivid scarlet coloured hair that resembled them being fashioned out of a piece of velvet. I think they may have been one of the largest species of mite that inhabit the earth. We used stare in wonder at this God given moving red carpet. It was impossible not to walk on them. The stink bug and the blister beetle were nasty little horrors who when out with a torch at night would home in on the carrier. They did exactly as their nick-names imply. The first's smell was putrid and the second caused a huge swelling should it be inadvertently crushed on the skin.

I always wondered at the clouds of insects that were attracted to night lights, especially whenever I had to go to the airport in the evening. The number of species seemed legion. Where did they all go to in the daytime? One also had always to iron well every item of clothing that was put out to dry otherwise the tumbu maggot might take up residence in skin. Ironing killed it.

Mole Crickets made so much noise at night and if within 6-7 metres of a bedroom equivalent in decibels to a high pitched alarm. I had to wear ear defenders to dig out the first one that I had ever come across. He was half a metre down in a hole happily trying to attract a mate. It is the most horribly fashioned creature when placed on a hand, but perfectly harmless and this one I deposited 30 metres away in the hope we might get some sleep. Within 10 minutes he was back. Sadly, a live Mole Cricket meant no sleep. There was also no sleep when the figs in the tree overhanging the bungalow ripened, for this attracted the Fruit Bats. All night long there was their incessant chatter and the 'Ping-Pong' of the half eaten fruit they dropped onto the tin roof. Similar insomnia occurred when young monitors decide to hold midnight races in the roof space.

However life was just a matter of simple precautions and if certain rules were obeyed both at home and in the field there were never any problems, except for mosquitoes. They were always an incessant problem. No matter what my erstwhile medical colleagues think, and they were eminently qualified, I am convinced a mosquito smells a new arrival to Africa at a thousand paces. I am also convinced, as a natural defence, the body builds up something obnoxious to the mosquito that is excreted in the perspiration of an 'old sweat'. Newcomers were driven mad, while the old hands seemed to be able to sit out on the veranda at night, but only after two years of service. However, to counteract these pests we used to place buffalo dung rings at the perimeter of any occasion at night and the smell of these either drove the mosquitoes or the newcomers away. We got used to it.

I will always remember our Christmas Eve outdoor praise sessions with the family around a campfire in the garden of our bungalow, singing carols to the accompaniment of our son John's guitar and the smell of burning dung. I also remember one morning getting up early and on entering the lounge noticing that light only appeared to be entering from one side of the room. Closer inspection revealed that there were so many mosquitoes attached to the screens over the windows that the light had been blotted out. It was like a blanket had fallen off the screen when I tapped the window. Later on I found that our bungalow had been built on the edge of a reclaimed swamp! Other than this, mornings were my favourite times. To be in Africa, shortly after dawn was joy beyond belief, before the sun baked everything. It was so fresh with a plethora of God's creatures singing their welcome to a new day.

The terrain

Living in the suburbs was not too bad. There were roads of description and where these became impassable, due to a new crater being formed, one simply drove off the road and then back on. This was perfectly acceptable, even with the owner of the bit of land. Occasionally the roads were mended. This meant that some charitable institution like the British Government, or the World Bank, had supplied funds for the renewal. The work would start and continue in fits and starts, owing to funds being 'creamed off' until half-finished it was left in a state that would cause maximum chaos to the population. Those who had lined pockets would fire the ex-patriot engineers as scape-goats and another benefactor would step in and complete the road for a tenth of the price, which meant the road surface had only one layer of asphalt. At the next onset of rains the road fell away in places and pot holes reappeared. This process was repeated ad-nausea for the whole time I was in the region. This explanation is not an indictment but merely a statement of fact regarding the country I was resident in. Just like much of the rest of the world there was extreme corruption and the history book informs the traveller that many of Africa's colonial masters were in fact experts in this line of business.

Driving on bush roads was interesting providing excitement for a 'four by four' vehicle. On the sea side of the country it could run into sudden dunes, but otherwise the ground consisted of a mixture of hard packed red dust or desert rock. Driving in the actual bush was exhilarating as it proved difficult to navigate but there were always native travellers only too willing to point out the right direction. Bush is as it says. It could be thick at times but was often sparse and it was intermittently populated by trees. In the hot season to be caught in bush fire was not much fun and twice I had to outrun such a fire and on several occasions take detours.

The country was dominated by a large river which was always a delight to get onto and bathe in, especially in the hot season. So long as flowing water was chosen the swimmer was relatively safe from contracting Bilharzia, a particularly foul infestation.

Journeys up and down country were a joy to me. There was always that added excitement if the adventurer was on their own, but then I never was. Journeys to the three other countries I had to drive to or through were adventures every single trip, especially when it was not known who was fighting with whom in the area, or whether a road or embarking point on a river had been washed away. I once had to drive miles into heavy tropical bush to rescue a man who was reported as being injured. We did not often do this but The Lord saw this as important on this occasion, so I burned up valuable time and fuel getting there. Eventually locating the small village and the patient, he presented me with compound fracture of one leg. He was friendly but vociferous and was completely drunk on palm wine. There was no need for an anaesthetic to get him patched up and into the Land Rover and even after an hours journey to a local hospital, he reported that his leg was 'beginning to ache.' He turned out to be the off duty Police Chief of the country and the story he related was illuminating. My gentleman, who had fallen out of the tree, had got up there simply to get away from his wife's nagging. He had purposely taken a jar of wine up into the tree to get drunk, but further argument caused him to lose his footing. On reaching the ground he called for more anaesthetic to drink. He was a powerful man, and spoke excellent English. Now at the time we were painstakingly negotiating with the local government to set up a laboratory in the region, to study a village where all the elderly residents seemed

HIV immune. The red tape was testing us to destruction but after mentioning the problem to my tree squirrel we got our permission for the lab in a week. I was actually setting it up 'in advance' of permission and it was virtually completed so we were able to start work immediately. It is truly amazing how The Lord arranges the order of things. Nothing is a waste of time and material if He is brought into the scheme of everything.

The Suburban Western African

Let me say that no matter what the above local African tried to do to me; no matter how he managed to wind me around his little finger, I loved him like a brother. I did not, and do not profess to understand his ways and often had to turn my back on many of his practices but there was something infectious about him that kept me laughing right up to the end. Importantly he was also willingly put up with me!

There is no doubt that any tourist to the country would have been plagued to some degree by local youths all trying to sell a service or a thing. Even when highly annoyed it was quite impossible to shake them off and somewhere down the line a few coins would exchange hands to stop the pestering. All through the protractor would have been polite and would crack jokes and would give such a grin that it just had to be returned. Often the individual would tell a 'sob' story. It would feature the desperate plight of members of his family and how a set of unfortunate circumstances have prevented him from carrying on with his education and that he was looking for sponsorship of any kind. The story would only have contained a grain of truth, but they are the experts at hustling.

Professional hustlers abounded and always succeeded, because the tourist always had so much as compared with the African and in any case as they were on holiday, they felt guilty. The tourist always felt good to share and if pestered too much they knew they would at most be home in 10 days. It was different for us as we lived here. I fell afoul of 'con' men, once losing my entire months expenses for the mission.

The African 'tried it on', as he trudged many a mile alongside me. Before he knew me, he did his utmost to extort something from my pocket. We would discuss everything from Imperialism to current affairs in Africa, on which he always had an opinion and he would always tell me the world was much better off under the British. Inevitably we got onto Christianity which would then lead onto Islam and eventually I would expose his real religion, which was some form of spirit worship and that usually ended the conversation. I never told him to go away and I never told him I was ever better or worse off than him and so trudging around the suburbs of the capital, I developed a reputation of being the man 'who wanted to talk.'

I had decided upon arrival to always wear the cross of Jesus on the collar lapel of my shirt. I took Jesus everywhere so no one was in doubt as to who or what I was. Soon it was interesting to note that I was recognising certain hustlers and they were actually taking time out of their precious day to philosophise with me. This was good. Naturally I did try to help them out from time to time but I always tried to give them what they needed and not what they wanted. If they said money was for food then we went to a shop and bought some. If the truth was that they needed it for cigarettes, then this would come out in front of the shopkeeper. The next time when they wanted money for cigarettes they stood a better chance of getting it from me. As I got known, the demands increased and became desperate for those who were in desperate circumstances. I tried to do my best within my own personal budget. Much of my giving to the locals initially centred on the Institute hospital to which I was attached.

The suburban native family lived in shanty town accommodation. A building consisting of breeze blocks with a tin roof and the size of the average U.K. living room would house at least four people. One building seemed to be built into another. Often the buildings had two rooms. One was designated for the mother and father and the other for everyone else, which could include children, grandparents, relatives and any itinerant. Toilets were often open sewers and privacy was non-existent. Incest was fairly common and general fornication rampant. Drugs were also fairly common but interestingly alcoholism was rare, but it was a Muslim country. A large nut was purchased openly in the streets and chewed by many during the day. I think this was the Kola, but whatever it was it definitely created some sort of buzz which kept people going during the day.

Bread was eaten for breakfast along with tea. If another meal was eaten during the day it was in the evening and consisted of rice and usually fish with vegetables. Meat was eaten only on special occasions. Everyone tried to drink water wherever they went. The African male was lean, muscular and very fit but when I was there the thought of getting AIDS was getting him down. The wife spent the day in the compound doing practically everything. She would wash clothes, get water, prepare food, and look after the needs of everyone. She often had a little side job selling something in a nearby market. She would also be the administrative head in all matters. The husband if he did not work, or was too old or apathetic to hustle, stayed away from her as much as he could and whiled away his time in the shade, by talking about nothing in particular. In the evening he could hustle around trying to get some cigarettes, beer or a meal. He did not care too much what happened at the compound during that day. He came home to sleep and to get up the next day to restart the process. The families, whose men worked, were better off. Landlords were extortionate by nature and very few people owned their buildings, which by our standards could be built for a couple of hundred pounds.

The West African villager

To go out to the villages was a treat. There was a headman and the hierarchy of the village spread out from him like an umbrella. He was the law. The average local in the village was somewhat reticent to meet with a white visitor. They were naturally suspicious and rarely spoke any English. They lived a different kind of day to his counterpart in the towns as there was land or animals to tend to and earn a living. Basically they scratched out an existence. The buildings were mud baked brick with thatched fronds for a roof and were circular instead of rectangular. If the family was prosperous they could revert to breeze block and tin. Most were not prosperous. A wife however did exactly the same as her counterpart in the city however she also had to work in the fields, which was an extra burden. The village African did not have the cheekiness of his counterpart and knowledge of the weaknesses of the 'Tubab' (white man) was not so widely understood. If the villager knew the person wanted to offer help he was very grateful and if known personally he would share everything he had. I liked him. He was far more trustworthy than his counterpart in the town and we needed his co-operation for all the research work that needed to be carried out.

Unfortunately the village African was often suffering in some way or another depending on what particular calamity befell the village. Drought and pestilence along with accompanying malnutrition were as common place as malaria. He needed clinics to be set up to combat these conditions and a deal of sympathy. A villager looked forward to a visit but rarely saw any tourist unless it was someone trying to trace their roots.

Modesty was never a problem and that was something the ex-patriot and the missionary had to get used to. Life was very cheap and a baby could be purchased cheaply with ease or even a young girl to be a slave, or worse. Unfortunately there was many an occasion when I could have compromised everything I stood for. Girl babies were relatively unimportant as compared to boys in both African and Islamic culture, and a most cruel practice was to take an unwanted child and just leave it on its own in the bush, or even simply not feed it. This as ghastly as it sounds, was simply the way in this part of Africa. If questioned the mother would say that she could not keep the child as the father did not want it; so God would have to look after it in the bush.

The village was always firmly in the grip of the Marabout or witchdoctor who would carry out spells and issue charms for life. The religion was mixture of Islam and spiritualism. For example the mystic jujus carried on a person would be in the form of little leather purses which often contained verses of the Koran. The Imams were always battling against local 'pagan' beliefs. The Marabout was responsible for most of the terror that took place inside the local African's mind. Driven by satan he or she's control was complete, through fear. These individuals were to become my greatest adversary in my walk for Jesus and praise God, often defeated, in dramatic style by the power of His Spirit.

I would not want to close this section on anything but my love and respect for the village native I came across but I shall leave it with a tale of African stoicism. One day I received a call on the radio that one of our vehicles was broken down in some rough country and needed assistance. As I was attending the donated Chinese hospital up country and as I was the nearest to the vehicle I said I would go and recue the occupant. It was a journey along uncharted territory and I remember travelling down a long track cutting through some paddy fields. After a while a bullock cart was seen coming towards me and we eventually met.

The driver I guessed was in his 60's, and I greeted him and asked where he was from and where he was bound. He said he had been on the road for two days and was going to the Chinese hospital from whence I had come. His wife was sick and he was taking her for treatment. I asked him if I could help by examining her, for I always carried some emergency medicines. When I told the old man his wife was dead he did not show any emotion but thanked me profusely for my efforts and slowly and skilfully turned the bullock cart around in the narrowest of passage-ways and headed home.

I stood there for some time crying. I did not know why at first but realised it was for his tragedy and that of Africa, the human race, poverty, and our selfishness in the west. His acceptance and bravery stunned me so much that I just wanted to run after him and hug him. I cannot get this memory out of my mind, nor do I really ever want to. It reminds me of my fortune. How I eventually retrieved my senses, repassed his cart on the narrow road to get to my stranded colleague is another story.

Chapter 4: The Mission Church

St Peters, the church at Jafara where I was stationed and which catered for no more than fifty souls, was on the coast and had between five and twenty years left in existence before plunging down the cliff into the sea. 'Sea Eagle point' was not more than 30 metres away from the building but almost certainly the church does not exist as I write. It was made of brick and had a steel roof and was interesting for one aspect. The church greeted any visitor upon entering with the sight of an ominous crack running down the middle of the central aisle and then up the back wall of the building. It did not take much intelligence to realise that the church was actually splitting in two, right down its middle. Each year a certain amount of concrete was poured in to seal up the crack in the floor and wall, which appeared to re-open in only a matter of weeks. I always had this vision that one day, when preceded by a violent creaking sound and cloud of dust, the church would gently cleave itself; the two halves coming to rest in a sort of V shape. Then out of the 'chrysalis' would arise a small army of black arms raised to the skies, to be followed by the bodies that owned them, all drifting slowly up to heaven. I do not usually get smitten by prophetic visions, but who knows?

The building had a nice little altar, communion rails and chairs with hassocks. At the front was the vestry, that contained all the usual paraphernalia and the whole set up was very Anglican. Outside was found one great round and thatched building for extra church activities. The buildings overlooked the sea, which gave members of the congregation a pleasant and breath-taking distraction during boring sermons. We followed the prayer book to the letter and sung good old solid Anglican type hymns. It was nicely conservative in worship. Occasionally someone sneaked in a set of Mission Praise books which usually raised eyebrows and some form of criticism, but on the whole it was sensible and well organised with due reverence to God. He would have been well pleased with the order shown. There was no sign of the Holy Spirit, but the place was heavy on respect which was very proper and very British.

There was one incumbent priest, who was part time and travelled some ten miles to and from his residence in the capital city. He also doubled as the mathematics master at the local native High School and was also very proper and very English. He was true blue, so to speak, and an inveterate bachelor (or so he thought) and had no problems in anointing a parishioner or their vehicle with Holy Water, if it was necessary for its safety. He was around six foot tall and weighed about nine stone. He had his devils which finally caught up with him later in life. I liked, and got on with Tom and so entered the world of the Anglican Church, which was to be my formative training in church affairs, and religion.

The Aku

I have to tell the story about the people who formed the majority of the congregation. They were African and they were black but they belonged to a very unusual minority tribe. The African is very proud of his heritage and it is extremely important to him to know exactly where his roots lie. Today, he tolerates someone from another tribe, however before colonialism he was perpetually at war with his neighbour.

It was considered a normal part of life to go and raid the territory of an adjoining tribe, or even that of a splinter group of one's family. Those who were successful in their raids became more powerful and rich than their neighbours, as they carried off vast amounts of booty from their conquests, which were often bloody. For centuries Arab slavers plied the coast followed by Europeans and much later many natives found themselves on ships bound for America and Britain. Contrary to popular belief, it was not the latter day slavers who rounded up the natives for deportation but always one notable tribe in the locality. Having warred since time immemorial against their allotted enemies, they had no compunction when 'white' men arrived in huge ships to offer them money to haul their vanquished into captivity, rather than slaughter them. The pictures of traders plundering villages in many regions are mostly untrue. They simply dropped anchor in the bay and negotiated a treaty with the most forceful tribe around, however should the quotas not tally at the end of the day, the traders would then take their former partners on board for the adventure.

The British finally colonised the place after seeing off any other European interest and established an island trading post for their evil trade. When slavery was abolished in America, all the Africans en-route or in transit camps were shipped back and disembarked in West Africa. A new city sprung up which is today the capital of Sierra Leone. It was and is, aptly called Freetown. After arrival they were completely disorientated and had no idea where or how far away their homelands were. The locals, if not hostile, were totally ignorant of their needs and into this melting pot came a whole succession of missionaries. (I say succession as most of them only lasted a short time before dying). They came to give desperate people some hope and for many that hope was Jesus.

United by religion, the old memories and prejudices died away and the Freetown Africans organised themselves into an intelligentsia. Having more links with their new 'masters' than with anyone else, they soon provided the 'white collar' workers for the colonialists. They took posts in civil and public service. Descendants of these people still bear names that indicate the favour given them at some stage in their lives. Surnames such as George, Henry and Smith are common. So the Aku tribe was born and the congregation of the Jafara Mission Church comprised mainly Aku with a sprinkling of white people, but not one indigenous African was present when I joined it.

My family and I settled down to comfortable Anglicanism, with a dash of Baptist worship thrown in. Southern Baptists, as the name implied were from the deep south of America in what I always believed was staunch conservative Christianity of the kind I found later in South Africa. Meeting the folks in Africa confirmed my belief to be correct. We were accepted and at worst politely tolerated, as we were not of that ilk, but were allowed to attend the evening service for a year. I think to begin with we were an oddity, if not embarrassment in asking to join with them. No one usually would do such a thing unless belonging to that denomination.

Once having missed three Sundays running, due to an up country trip and illness, we found that on turning up at the appointed time for the evening service at their mission church, no one else was there. After repeating this fruitless exercise on the following Sunday, we drove straight to a pastor's home. He politely informed us that as we had not turned up for the three Sundays running, they had cancelled the evening service, as they had only kept it going for us. We were mortified. It was flattering and delightful that the services had continued because of us, but also disturbing. What strange policy allowed them to have continued in this fashion? I still puzzle over this. But I will always remember the singing. Everyone at this mission could read music and through the practice in their churches over many years could harmonise. Whenever I hear 'It is well with my soul,' I will always think of them. Their rendition brought tears to my eyes and filled my heart to bursting.

One of our problems, which metered out to me by the Bishop designate and also by a Baptist lay Pastor, was that we should not openly embrace other Christians in other denominations, nor attend their churches. It was simply not done. Whenever I posed the question as to why not, I never got an answer, only the knowing smile. I realised that my wife and I were actually shaking the pillars of tradition. The denominations worked in many villages, some for example looking after wells while others handed out food, but I noticed the various works were not allowed to overlap, due to the embarrassment of doctrinal beliefs. Is this really the best way to carry out the grand Commission? It used to make me fume under the collar and I did my utmost to sabotage such insular behaviour, so I developed a reputation as being eccentric amongst the brethren. To me Christianity has nothing to do with denomination which I consider to be a very powerful tool of the devil. I am reminded of a cartoon I once saw in a Catholic Church newspaper many years ago. This was published in the days when Catholics believed that Protestants were all heretics and the Jews were responsible for killing Jesus. So it was a rather brave statement by the editor. Sadly the joke stands the test of time but today and any denomination could be substituted if there is a wish to retell the story with any particular bias. In this case, the scene showed an elderly couple walking in the garden of heaven. She has just joined him and is being shown around. She remarks how beautiful it all is but shows concern for a large walled off area in the centre. “Oh,” remarks her husband “don’t worry, the Catholics think they are the only people in Heaven”. Perfectly satisfied with the explanation the wife continues on her walk of discovery.

Why we continue to balk at the thought of changing tradition amazes me. Many within the church find it so difficult to accept that to be critical does not mean condemnatory. Who exactly did God trust to keep his word alive for the 2000 years since the birth of Jesus? Was not Luther a Catholic? Was not Wesley an Anglican? Was not Jesus a Jew?

So long as criticism is constructive and designed to turn situations back to Biblical teaching, there is never any problem, however many churches still cannot accept this. A classic example of someone who was highly critical and who turned everything upside down in his ministry was Jesus himself and I marvel when I overhear Christians discussing as to which place He would go to if he visited their locality. I tell them he would not visit any church, but would probably stroll down to the local pub or supermarket. So it was that I developed an undeserved reputation as being truly eccentric. Although I did not know it at the time I had been also ear-marked as a trouble-maker. This label has been attached to me on and off for years ever since and sometimes I have to look to my laurels to believe I am on the right track. I thank God that, more often than not, He tells me I am.

Unfortunately the net result of such a distancing in Africa eventually led to ostracism, jealousy, envy, bitterness and malice. I hasten to add that none of this was from me, well very little, anyway. However, this is quite a list to encourage the 'would be' missionary or travelling ecumenicist, but please do not be too alarmed. Let me say this, if anyone should be active for God they will meet with the greatest opposition within the confines of the church. This is especially so if signs and wonders follow the preaching of the word, but then if He is for us then who could be against us. Let me make a point clear. I only advocate ecumenism in its simplest practical form, such as everyone working together in the mission field. Having our own delineated areas and barriers is pathetic and confusing to the pagan, however where doctrine is contrary to the Bible, that is where I draw the line. In addition outside the world of Christianity we do not serve the same God. To say that Yahweh and Allah and are one and the same person can only be born out of frightening ignorance.

On another matter, should a discreet ministry be practiced then this would be considered highly acceptable practice as it would not interfere with society. Handing out alms is fine and worthy whereas preaching may be frowned upon and even considered seditious. Any new ministry has to gain respect from existing Christian leaders of all denominations to obtain toleration by any government of the country where residency is sought. It is good job that Jesus Christ did not consider any of these matters when he started his ministry. However if in evangelising on behalf of this Jesus Christ the proverbial applecart is overturned so consciences are pricked, then the organisation and the troublemaker will find out who their friends are and whether their brand of religion is really as tolerated in the country as the tourist brochure claims it to be. If this sounds a little cynical at this stage please wait to see what unfolds, but let us never forget that Jesus brought a sword and not peace to the world. (Matthew 10:34) He meant that the truth will only bring separation and enmity. Jesus and the Apostles were anything but unobtrusive. If it is considered sheer stupidity to upset the authority in a country as Jesus did, let us also remember that he was so devout and lovely in his mission to the people even the thief on the cross recognised his innocence. Today we commend ourselves for our sense of equality and diversity which is nothing but hypocrisy. We actually mean we must have equality and diversity unless someone comes and tells us they are different, in which case we must hate them. Jesus said he was the Son of God and a fulfilment of the law and they hated him for it. I said I was a disciple of Jesus Christ who has called me to be his messenger to set you free and they hated me for it. There is no difference in the hatred only in the divinity of the former.

Regarding our tolerance of each other today, it would surprise the average believer to discover who is either suing or condemning whom, in the evangelical leadership around the world. We all seem to be jealous of a successful evangelist and are determined to expose the individual at any cost. Not that I am saying that many do not need exposing, but the job of a watch-keeper is to bring to the attention of the church the commandments and warnings given by Jesus Christ. It is the people who matter. They each have the right and the choice to decide whether their church or leader is of God or not, by matching what is said or done with scripture. We can point out errors, but it is God who will determine the fate of people. We are not allowed to name them but point out bad behaviour and practices and we certainly should never find ourselves in court unless it is because we are accused of being a born again Christian. How can we actually sue another person even if they should defame us? He suffered death on a cross and then asked the Father to pardon the executioners.

To simple folk like us the message is clear and it is to press on, to trim those wicks and keep that light shining for others. This I feel is more important today than at any time. At the risk of boring a lot of people, there are too many signs abroad to show that we are knocking at the door of the end times, so in my opinion wherever the mission field may be, or about to be, let us consider exactly what constitutes mission. Some people will say a Christians should live every day as though it is their last. I believe it is better to live it as though it is the first, then possibly there would be less room for mistakes..

Back at Jafara, the family settled into the way of life in the Anglican Church. Because we were on fire for The Lord, I was soon helping in the vestry and organising a weekly prayer group and for several months with my wife running the Sunday school with another ex-patriot lady, at which I assisted from time to time. This school was an absolute joy. The children had little idea of what it was to be a Christian and through stories, mime, drawings and gentle coercion, the times spent in that round hut outside the church were some of the happiest we experienced in Africa.

We really got somewhere with these children. Unfortunately all good things have to come to an end and we were forced to cease our activities, which sadly heralded the eventual closing of the whole Sunday school. Objections were made to the P.C.C. about our teaching and free thinking. One example of a complaint was that we taught the children that Christian families should read the Bible and pray together each day...and yet they met every day in the Temple. (Acts 2:46) As this was never practiced in that community such a statement by the leaders of the Sunday school was considered seditious. We had openly criticised the parents!

The Parochial Church Council, PCC, is the elected governing body of an Anglican church. I would wish that everyone should serve on one at least once in their lifetime just for the experience. I had become a member because I had put my name down for a place in the forthcoming inaugural Bible teaching course at the School of Evangelism. This was at the Cathedral in the capital. I had not asked permission of the incumbent priest at the Jafara church which I should have done, but had been accepted on the course as they had presumed no-one would be in their right mind to apply if they had not the backing of their own parish priest. I had neglected this in ignorance and zeal and for no other reason. Anyway they could not retract and Tom thought it an excellent idea anyway, and so I was on my way to Bible College. However, being a trainee Lay Reader meant it would be rather incongruous if I was not admitted to the PCC. And so I attended the meetings. I have never experienced anything like it for an exercise in self-control. I could not believe how it was possible for apparently God fearing folk to metamorphose into vessels of pompous vested interest during the week. It was a tremendous shock to my embryonic Christianity. The biggest part of this was to discover this wretched behaviour was acceptable, especially the elders, including Tom. It was the norm for such meetings. I used to wonder why Tom always developed a nervous tick at the mention of the PCC, and now I knew why. An example of an important item on the agenda of a meeting would be the organisation of a social event. An example of an unimportant item would be anything remotely spiritual. The Lord was teaching me fast about the dark side of church life and so I, metaphorically, threw myself into my studies.

The students on the course at the school of evangelism, attended three nights a week, with interspersed week end seminars, which included the duties of both controlling and being part of, the various Anglican services. We were taught everything about the Bible, how to read music, how to chant responses and where and when to bow and show respect to elders and the like. At a dedication service we were visibly humbled and over-awed at the sight of the only two existing lay readers in the diocese who were presented to us. Suitably gowned and 'medalled' they went through their paces with an impressive air of pomp and ceremony, when all the while, the Bishop sat on his throne in splendid regalia. When I now think back to this time, I have great difficulty in believing it all took place in this century, or rather that is how it appears in my mind's eye. Anyway adequately anointed I felt encouraged. I wanted to become a 'super reader' but, I was the only white face on the course.

Back at Jafara I was encouraged to take parts and then all of the services. When preaching the word it was nothing but enthralling. I was as happy as anyone could possibly be in my life enthusing over every beautiful day, event, and service and could not understand why others did not feel the same, when they congregated. I threw myself into organisation, spent a lot of energy in forcing members to meet and love each other and particularly those who were less fortunate or belonged to other denominations. In short I became a pain in the neck. Frustration set in and after yet another puzzling incident I decided to take stock of my situation. I realised that although I was madly in love with Jesus, due to my instant conversion, other people were not enamoured the same way; yet another shock to add to the growing list. Why do people not love Jesus as much as I do? I had to seek counsel from Tom and he pointed out many things to me. I learnt about the argument regarding what constitutes 'salvation' and the fact that although Jesus asked us to tell others about the good news the main job was to make disciples of those within the church. "Who are the disciples in our church?" I asked. He just smiled at me. He did add that everything was up to The Lord and I should stop striving and gently go with the swell. This seemed contradictory and was the beginning of a path of serious questioning as to what exactly Jesus wanted from us when he left the earth. Had we got it all wrong? After meditating on this subject, a lot of fog was removed from my newly spiritual mind by this conversation. I realised exactly what it was that God wanted from me. He wanted me to strive to make disciples of men and definitely not go 'with the swell'. I also realised what the Bible meant when it spoke about many being called but few are chosen, but was I chosen for leadership? I wanted to find out what that meant.

The Bible course proceeded and the most significant observation concerning the tutorials and teaching sessions was the poor attendance. In Africa time is of relative importance and to turn up within half an hour of an allotted start of any event is considered reasonable. When it rains no-one turns up at all and when there is the slightest excuse for a holiday break, then everything stops. Does God go on holiday? Homework began to be handed in later and later and projects were rarely completed on time. All this behaviour I found irksome and voiced my opinion, which created inevitable tension. On one occasion I was told in front of the class that if I did not like how things were being organised then I should go home; the first, albeit slight, reference to my ethnic origin and yet another hurtful shock to add to the list. I hungered and thirsted for righteousness and found I could simply not back down and 'go with the swell.' If something was worth doing, it was worth doing well for God. The others saw no particular need.

In class I was always the questioner, and the one who wanted to get under the skin of the character in the Bible. As far as the college was concerned I continued to be a thorn in the side of ignorance, but I learned the art of tolerance in the face of increasing racism. I suffered this in reverse and had to overcome many a test, but to my credit I understood the reaction without prejudice on my part. Who was I to complain after our dubious history in the place? 'God grant me the serenity to accept the things I could not change, courage to change the things I could, and wisdom to know the difference.' (Anonymous saying)

My true feelings about Christian attitude spilled over in one seminar which nearly got me thrown out of the college. The Bishop was teaching us that day, which was a rare event. He was expounding on the traditions and relics of the church, pouring through history and stressing the profound differences that existed between Anglicanism and any other denomination but became aware of my obvious distaste. He suddenly rounded on me. I had still little idea why I was being tested.

"Grummitt, what would you do if you had been sent to the hospital to give communion to a dying Anglican and in the process of this the man in the next bed, who was also dying, but neither a parishioner or known believer, called out to receive the sacrament?"

Without hesitating I said "I would give it to him of course."

This sent the Bishop into the biggest fit I had ever seen him in. He ranted and raved at me about my false beliefs in such a way that stunned everyone present. He finished by saying "And you call yourself an Anglican?" I answered, "I don't Bishop. I call myself a follower of Christ." The blue touch-paper for being fired from the course was lit. It was to burn slowly.

The Bishop turned as purple as his dress and promptly left the room. My fellow students rounded on me and were not too kind about the fact that I had ruined the lesson for them.

Due to intervention by others I managed to survive the incident and the whole course and even the final exams, which I passed along with two others. The remainder had failed but there was an unsavoury twist to the whole saga, and a distinct possibility the Bishop was heavily involved in what took place. In the policy document, we signed at the start of the course, it stated that no student would be allowed to pass unless they had attended 75% of all lectures. In fact only two students out of the original thirteen had the requisite record of attendance; namely the two which actually passed. The senior lecturer, who had brought this anomaly to the attention of the senate, was none other than my old friend Dr Smith, who was also a 'resting' Lay Reader from the U.K. His speciality was the Old Testament, the intricacy of which he taught with zeal during our term.

The disaster for the Bishop could not be greater? This was the flagship course for lay readership in the whole Diocese and should have been a personal triumph for the Dean of the school, but only two people had passed, according to their self-imposed regulations and embarrassingly one was white. I am not suggesting for one moment that what happened next had anything to do with racism, but their dilemma was to find a way to salvage a situation when one of the only two who graduated was a native. The well-advertised passing out service was going to be sparsely attended by graduates. The Bishop called all the candidates together and informed us that due to a very low achievement level, a future six months of study was needed to bring everyone up to the required academic standard. In order to avoid embarrassment to the church all students would carry on with the extended course work. However, there was to be one exception to his command as the one African colleague, who passed alongside me, was immediately instated as a lay reader attached to the Cathedral. I was asked to continue. At the end of the extension six more graduated and the six had their photos in the press, alongside the existing cathedral lay reader. There was one notable absentee as far as I was concerned. I was also the only one never to receive my accreditation. Before all this happened both I, as a student and Dr Smith, as a lecturer, resigned from the course, for obvious reasons. They had no other lecturer to take his place. On my part, as matters turned out I had little time to reflect on this dreadful situation for I was soon to be very busy. When now I have time to reflect on what happened I only want to remember my good times at the school, and my colleagues who I did my best to befriend and encourage. If my colleague had not been appointed to serve at the cathedral both he and I would have been glad to 'serve out' the six months. The blatant discrimination precluded this.

My resignation from the course must have been too much for Tom, for he immediately contracted a serious bowel condition and had to be flown to England for treatment, which lasted 11 months. The irony of the situation was that the Bishop was forced to make me the Lay Reader and Official in Charge of the Jafara Church, which probably appeased his conscience and made me overjoyed. The Lord works in wondrous ways and He wanted my training to be completed for this purpose. God has no interest in the award of a piece of paper and a medal of office, nevertheless both were withheld and never awarded, even after the 11 months of service within the diocese. However this gave me ample reason to leave the mission, not that I needed it. However, at the time of Tom's departure I immediately warmed to my new role by unwittingly whittling down the congregation. Dismayed as I was to see it diminishing I was very heartened that the numbers at the prayer group increased. Following its inception I had often been the only one in the church, week after week. I put it down to the fact that God liked quality and not quantity? One sad loss was the British High Commissioner and his wife, who never really forgave me over one sermon on the evils of serving mammon. However it was very comforting to notice that some people were actually beginning to move in the Spirit. They always had him in their hearts but now they felt free to express their emotions in the church and I was learning a great deal, through this season of my life, that God only wants quality. Someone once told me of a story of a new ordained curate who, when asked whether he had been assigned to active church, replied 'Most assuredly as my church is extremely active. Half the church is actively for me and the other half is actively against me.'

I served this church as its priest for nearly a year and thoroughly enjoyed it but committed four great misdemeanours. Firstly I upset the organist, of twenty years standing, by gently insisting that we should stick to the hymns pertinent to the delivered sermon. (This apparently was none of my business, as Tom related his sermon to the hymns suggested by the organist!) Secondly I banned alcohol from inside the church but refuse to give any further explanation. Thirdly I refused to bless inanimate objects and lastly I introduced pastoral visits. Of these four, the most damaging to my standing within the church was the upsetting of the organist. He was later awarded an OBE for his services to the Anglican community in West Africa and called at my bungalow to boast of his award. The Queen apparently appreciated him even if I did not. Bless him!

On the plus side the shortened version of the services were now standard, along with Mission Praise song books and the congregation started to be much freer in praise. I did not banish everything but kept all the old traditions, like marching around the church on Palm Sunday waving huge palm leaves and praying for people and making a fuss of them on their birthday and giving mention of family success and joy in the notices. I decided that there was a lot to be said about keeping good solid traditions and I often feel that the 'happy-clappy' brigade may have been too hasty to get rid of them all. Can we not learn from each other? One disappointment was my failure to get the PCC to reinstate the Sunday school.

I spent a lot of my time introducing myself to other denominations apart from the Southern Baptists and we made friends with Methodists, Catholics, and a lovely Korean Pastor and his wife. We occasionally had fellowship with a number of emergent evangelical groups, all of whom seemed to stammer in tongues at the slightest provocation. My motives were probably selfish as opposed to any ecumenical desire. I wanted to meet them all, in order to find out what they believed in and what they got out of their brand of religion, and what they thought of other Christians. I had a relatively successful time introducing some thoughts on my basic ecumenism into their lives, along the lines of just serving Jesus Christ in the mission field. However, the old bigoted views re-emerged and everything slowly reverted back to the hard line doctrines and delineated areas of work. Jesus makes things so simple yet man makes them so difficult, through his pride.

In the mean time I was to do a lot of walking around the neighbourhood. I was meeting people in their homes. I started praying for people to get healed of various conditions and situations and they did and so I started meeting my enemy first hand.

Chapter 5: Missionaries

I wonder just what the picture of a missionary might be when conjured up in the mind and what possibly might constitute the environment they would work in, maybe with his topi, shorts and Bible tucked beneath the arm?

There are many of us who have listened to the testimonies of people who have worked in the mission field, but we are often confronted in our churches by a neatly suited person extolling the virtues of such work and sadly, very rarely telling us how it really is, for the message is usually centred around what God is doing in that particular part of the Globe. Please do not misunderstand me for the fact that God works is nothing short of being wonderful, but what I am suggesting to the reader is that giving a one sided message not only fails to encourage others to follow in the missionary's footsteps, but at best it is only half the story. Why do I suggest it fails? Well, the missionaries that I have seen able to set heart's on fire in a meeting, are those who tell stories of deprivation, hardship, toil and sweat and then describe how all these had to be overcome to get God's work done. The audience is spellbound with the challenge. 'Yes' says the listener, 'Dear Lord I want to ride with you and help you blaze your trail in the face of the enemy?' That is how Hudson Taylor would do it! The reason why is because when the hearer compares the story of the individual back to scripture it becomes alive being similar to the journeys of the Apostles. Then, they want to go. But also let us remember Jonah did not want to go, but when he found God had ultimately removed the challenge from him he complained! (Jonah: 4)

Jesus tells us that we must pick up our cross and follow him daily and he also tells us constantly that we must overcome. Is this not more pertinent when in the field? If not, then I cannot imagine where else it could be. Of course it could be argued that are we not all in the field 'per se'. If that is the case and our lives are being lived out in abject comfort then is not something either terribly wrong with ourselves or the word of God?

Missionaries who only paint a glowing picture of innumerable conversions, in my opinion have somehow lost all sense of reality in their zeal. Many forget that 'coming to The Lord' involves a change of heart, soul and body and that Jesus did not ask us to go out and 'convert' but 'spread The Word and make disciples of men.' Whenever I hear a story of hardship or a testimony that relates to a fantastic spiritual battle that has to be waged, where the Lord through His grace brings a human vessel out of the mire, I literally cry for joy. This is the very substance of our beings as Christians. It is the stuff that disciples are made of and enables people to actually listen to what God is already whispering into their souls. It is the stuff that missionaries are born out of, when they, on hearing God's word, often sacrifice all else to go and do what He says. Then they are bound to be in the right place at the right time.

Missionaries come in many forms and what they are not, are statesman like icons clad in white tropical gear, keeping the scorching sun off their heads while they spend their time covering up the native from his nakedness, and giving him food. It is true that missionaries entice by administering a heavy dose of The Gospel to nourish the sick souls of the enquirers and in order to do this they have to be many things to different people. I can only talk about those I came across in my journey into life. What is not true is that all missionaries spread the Gospel, but I will expound on this later.

Argument continues as to the best way to equip a missionary while in the field. On one side the missionary, with or without his or her family, is catered for in the most abundant way, with a lot of the trimmings of home. On the other side this comfortable existence appears to be an anathema to the call, where the missionary it is felt should be no better off than the locals surrounding him, so creature comforts are kept to the minimum.

The first comprise the 'comfortable' Christian Mission groups which, when the going gets rough, can always retreat into their own world and be pampered. There are two problems these groups of Christians face. The first is having brought with them a supply of homely comforts, it will specifically highlight the social differences between their culture and that of the country they are living in. A second potential problem is that this situation causes a gradual increase in self-consciousness, as they are seen to be aloof. This may lead to a feeling of inadequacy in the field on one hand and an inordinate sense of failure and withdrawal on the other. Into this category also fall those who, having been convinced that they should go and do their bit for the Lord in the third world, find it so horrifying they not only retreat into their relatively safe havens whenever they can, but actually tick off the days until their term of contract is over. Usually they go through their hell on earth during their term. Sadly having gone to meetings at which some of them have spoken after coming home, I only hear the good things spoken of. This could ultimately lead to an increase in their sense of failure which, so I have been told, often leads onto a faith crisis. All this is due to being in the wrong place at the wrong time.

Not that the deprivation group do not have their own 'hang ups'. They suffer in different ways however for them there is no safe retreat to any creature comforts and so if they really are suffering, the ultimate reaction to all this is often a breakdown of health. Another problem within this group is that often, upon arrival, the missionaries will try to 'go native.' They do this either by adopting local dress or trying to copy local customs and traditions. It is a sad fact that most of these people open themselves up to ridicule, are considered eccentric in the extreme and fare very badly in their ultimate objectives. To try and understand the situation, imagine me as a supposedly BBC educated southerner in Britain, taking my family to live in some small northern Yorkshire village. Would we not quite rightly be considered as though we had just arrived from Mars? How many generations of the Grummitt family would have to live in that village before we were considered as being from 'rooned ere.' It can be imagine how this situation is multiplied in difficulty when there are ethical and cultural differences? Naturally I do apologise to any of those from Yorkshire reading this who may consider that there are exactly the same differences within the U.K., but in mitigation I hope that all get the drift of what I am trying to say. (This is especially so as I am now living in Stockton on Tees.)

I have even seen missionaries resorting to unacceptable practices within their own culture, such as hawking and spitting, in order to ingratiate themselves with the locals. This is somewhat ridiculous. The sad fact for these people, that I have discovered, is that a worker is more respected if they remain stay exactly as they are. The locals will find the missionary as fascinating as they are to the foreigner. The natives will learn to respect their customs as they will learn to respect the locals. It should be remembered as a foreigner, no missionary can ever become integrated within their own tribes, and they will never be open to ridicule by pretending to be what they are not. The missionaries who do not adapt the local ethnic baptism are the ones from whom the locals often enquire as to what makes them different from their colleagues.

There is another comic problem. Imagine a Scotsman, an American, a Korean, a Chinese and a Bolivian all trying to mimic the locals in dress and custom at an African village gathering? I doubt whether I could stand to be there for embarrassment. They are always the one's encouraged by the locals to go too far in the festivities and whereas these ex-patriots take their participation as a sign of acceptability they have no idea that the locals are thronging to see how they get on with performing, for example, the 'Chicken dance'. This is done often to their ridicule. Many a time I wished I had a camcorder handy for some of these gatherings for two reasons. One is to record the whole thing as an object lesson for the individual and the second would be to introduce the film back at home-base during a missionary teaching course, so that the humour and message would not be missed.

If I am upsetting those who have 'gone native' please also remember two important considerations. Firstly I can only report what I have seen and learned from my own mission, and secondly it is not my intention to hurt people, but simply to ask them to reflect on what it is they imagine they are achieving. I also realise I am generalising and there are exceptions to the rule in every circumstance, which will no doubt give some comfort, but for the would be missionary I hope this will give a good answer to the question as to how far anyone should go to become merged into the background. Respect for God's children and their ways is not an issue here. Learning the local language also does not fall into the category of advice above, but if it can be achieved it will be of enormous advantage. If like me there is difficulty in speaking English, let alone any native tongue, do not despair as necessity forces the assimilation of the language to at least be able to converse at the level of a 5-10 year old. This also is not a problem for many of the locals as due to a natural sense of the peculiar they will consider the missionary to be juvenile in most aspects of behaviour. After all what good are people who do not know how to skin a goat or identify component parts of a Jackfruit that are not edible, unless there is a wish to die? When understanding of such attributes is acquired by the missionary along with regard for important social behaviour, it will become clear that one's standing rises. However I am not advocating education in these matters before one 'goes out', well at least not in the former example!

Let us examine some of the groups that I came across where I will hope to paint a picture of what I saw, heard and conjectured. There is also an examination of the relative merits of the different way of doing things and I leave these observations as an open book for the reader to reflect on. I hope this will assist in any consideration while any seek God's guidance in the matter. Above all I hope to show that God moves in mysterious circles and somehow brings everything together. It's only us who mess it all up.

The first and most important point I will make is that if the mission field abroad is sought, when the motivation has been anything other than a direction from God the missionary will have the most miserable time they can imagine. Conversely, if God has ordered them to go, then the most satisfying of relationships with Jesus through the Holy Spirit will follow. This is despite snares that will be set by the enemy. God may require that person to be in situ forever or merely for a season, but this should never be an issue or a consideration regarding the calling. The missionary simply goes and waits on His instruction.

I want to satisfy in the mind as to how God will lead. Should the call come through a huge megaphone from Heaven saying "You are to give up your job, go into college and begin a life time's work as a missionary in Lapland," then all I can say is this is an enormous blessing. There should be not a waste of a moment in time before embarking on the calling. However, as in my case, there has to be a leading by the nose all the way, by a long suffering Father, then please be aware this is quite normal and there is no need to worry. Like me the process may have several stages, but the individual will always be aware of the calling.

This book is a record of how God spoke to me as a missionary and how I trusted Him at each stage to bring me through. It is meant to encourage at every stage. I will describe great hardships that came the way of my family and show that what happened during this season of service is as unforgettable to me as it will be of amazement to others. It should also encourage those who will always want to take any kind of leap of faith for The Lord. Although this took place thirty years ago the premise remains exactly the same.

Overseas Mission. (O.S.)

One always imagines Americans to be easy going, friendly, with just the right amount of reserve and so it was with the folk I met in Africa, as opposed to the British who are difficult, aloof, reserved and insular, or so I am told. The O.S. compound up country was truly something else to behold.

The first noticeable thing is that the whole is surrounded by a huge wire fence, tipped conveniently at the top with razors. The second is noticed upon entering that that everything within has been planned out and built to a professional standard, and not simply a collections of huts. These are manufactured from superb quality building materials which must have been brought into the country at great expense. There is an excellent generator house supplying quality air-conditioning as well as normal services, a well, garage for the 4x4 vehicles, a superb administrative building and even an equipped playground for the children. There is also a radio room and a huge mast with which the unit may independently communicate with the United States itself. The grounds, as such, are well kept by the gardeners and there is a security guard at the gate. The whole gives the impression of being a small well organised and well maintained exclusive village.

The missionaries within all had specific tasks to perform. The Head of the unit would be professionally qualified. When I visited he had a medical qualification of some description. Whatever the 'trade' of the Director, he was also in charge of all the administration as well as the main thrust of the work. In this case with this little outpost it was to sink wells in isolated villages. Everyone would beaver away but would meet up at regular intervals and the plans would be monitored and altered as necessary. Other members on the station would be support comprising mechanics, builders or technicians. Every morning the day would start with communal, non-compulsory prayers and every Sunday the group would worship in their own beautifully constructed chapel at which a small number of known locals would be allowed through the main gate, to attend. The overall impression was of a small well organised group of workers wherein each had specific roles and functions to perform. The impression was of everything being 'squeaky clean' in both appearance and attitude and after five years of knowing people in three such groups, and despite playing tennis with a friend who was member of one of these groups, I still never got to know what makes each one of them 'tick'. They were so good to me at times that it hurt and I wanted to just get away. At times they resembled the most perfect Christian families that I felt so humbled. At other times I wanted to pick each one up and shake them hard to see what would happen.

Whenever we got onto subjects that centred on evangelism and the work of The Holy Spirit, there would be offhand comments delivered in the nicest possible way. An example of this took place in the director's house whenever I introduced what they considered a contentious issue, where this would be greeted with "John and I have decided that we are not going to discuss such issues in this house." Strangely when this occurred it would almost certainly be followed by some remark as to my wellbeing. I got the impression, probably quite wrongly, that everyone was reverting to a pattern of behaviour learned as a form of catechism, at home-base. (How to talk to someone not of the same denomination)

The members of the O.S. mission were the first group I studied which led me to understand that, not all who are sent out as missionaries are evangelists armed with the Word of God as a sword. It shows how ignorant I was. My friend for example, who was an engineer, just engineered his term of contract. When it was over he went home as he completed his allotted time. Although a professed man of God he openly stated it was not his role to preach, counsel or evangelise, especially when he visited a village, as others in the mission station were brought over for that. He had spent two years in Africa and never once witnessed to a local, which I found extraordinary. To be fair he found my ignorance to be equally mystifying as my suggestion that we are all called to spread the word laughable, and countered quoting Paul's list of 'callings.' He was called to dig wells and that was that. He dug them, ticked off the days, and went back having run 'the course' that would ensure his better employment back home. I was shocked and he found me peculiar. When the time came for him to go home it was obvious that the nearer the date approached the more excited he became. He confirmed that he was glad he had done his time and it was over. He never understood why I felt so sad, both at losing a friend and for his obvious enthusiasm for going; although I never gave him satisfaction during the few games of tennis we played!

The Mission Head in one particular station was reading for his Ph.D. on Mission Work in Africa; his sole reason for being there. Needless to say I found very little evidence to equate with my own belief in the power of the Holy Spirit. Very little evangelising was carried out in their villages as compared with other groups, however a large number of villagers were very grateful for the first class wells that were dug and maintained.

Established Church Mission Number 1

The Anglicans (of which I was a member) took a very different attitude to exactly what was needed to bring people to God in that part of Africa. The up country stations were geared to helping the African to help himself. That is, to teaching him a trade in order that he might make sufficient money to keep both himself and his family. Occasionally he mistook the meaning of the term, but in theory it was an excellent project. In the time I frequented this mission station the workshops were plundered three times and a whole wealth of equipment was stolen on every occasion. Each time it was of course an inside job and the mission could, if they wished go and buy back the tools in the market the following day. They never saw the sense in doing so as it would be demeaning. They waited weeks for replacements to come out from England, while the few generally interested students, suffered hardship. In any case nobody really passed out on these courses because no-body really failed but worse still nobody really cared. The Missionaries were also simply too tired to care.

In studying the students I found out several salient facts. None of those I spoke to were in the slightest bit grateful to be given the opportunity to be at the mission, which surprised me. Only a few of them appeared to be living a decent form of Christian life and when I held up certain members as being examples of that ilk others used to snigger, which gave me a very bad feeling. There were fights in the dormitories which resulted in two being permanently closed. Drugs were rampant and alcohol played a big part in disruption of proceedings. To cap it all one of the incumbent priests thought nothing of having bare breasted girls in and around his compound as servants, which did nothing to enhance his particular standing with colleagues. This particular chap at every Sunday service at which he officiated, would prostrate himself before the altar at communion time and beat his breast fervently while repeating "Mea Culpa", over and over and over again; very disconcerting as it could only mean one thing. The same gentleman later left The Church altogether, when later as a leading candidate for a high office he was, to his surprise, turned down. His story was one of a completely burnt out missionary.

The compound resembled a broken down stage coach station in a wild-west movie. Anyone who pleased could walk in as the gates were permanently open. Whatever passed for a perimeter wall was, in parts easily ignored by walking through the wide gaps in its structure. The buildings were old and most had broken windows and holed roofs. The workshops and stores were often padlocked and barred while the whole place had a sense of decay. The missionary houses were small and without choice of air conditioning and also decayed. As the bush was unkempt around and about the whole place, it often encroached within. I loathed the place but loved the people.

One missionary couple in particular were good friends of mine. They ran a small-holding within the complex, teaching local students how to develop 'green fingers.' Their constant battle was with general apathy as they had to be behind every individual whether it was time for weeding or watering or general maintenance. They did grow some interesting vegetables, but on occasions these were simply purloined by two or four legged creatures and on one occasion when they went on leave they returned to find the whole 'farm' a total wreck. During this time the water pump on the well had broken down. They asked the students as to why no-one had resorted to using buckets for the plants. The answer is interesting. They received the merest shrug of the shoulders followed by silence. After all it meant extra work which had not been ordered. It did not matter to the students whether the plants were watered or not. It did not matter to them that the missionaries were distraught and it simply did not matter that they would have to start again from scratch. What it did show my friends that even the best students under their tutelage did not care whether the plants lived or died. This attitude has to be understood if mission is sought.

Against such odds I have seen missionaries reduced to sobbing and inconsolable grief. As to whether these local Africans realise that all this was for their benefit or not, remains unanswered. As to why the Christian converts in the group could not whip up enough enthusiasm to take over the job even in the stifling heat, remains a mystery to those who have toiled on their behalf for years, but it has to be remembered that no-one invited the missionary into the country and in coming he has to try and come to terms with hundreds and even thousands of years of fatalistic acceptance of tragedy and the '*will of God*' (Inshala!)

If the missionary, when confronted with such belligerence, can realise that all that can be done is to pick up their Cross on a daily basis and start all over again, then God would bless them indeed, even if achieved after a bit of ranting and raving. If the cross is lifted, the native will marvel and the missionary will leave behind a legacy that will have an effect. I fervently believe this. But it is difficult when driven to wits end. If the missionary can combine this with the love of Jesus then it is assured that somewhere down the line, at some other time and with some other person, the truth will dawn on the sinner and he or she will give their life to the Lord. How the missionary acts is important for it part of the legacy. Of this I have no doubt as no work done for The Lord is useless. My friends were a success story and triumphed eventually, but not until a lot of grief and hardship had been part of their work.

For years and although apparently healthy, they had tried to have a child. God granted them that child in His time, when they both had reached an understanding of purpose. This sounds very simplistic, but it is the basic truth of what did happen after a 'honing' by God on the anvil of Africa. I have no doubt wherever they might be today they would consider their initial work in this continent to have been of particular value in the conditioning of their lives.

There were others who suffered similarly who had nervous breakdowns and illnesses of degrees and who had to give up and go home. There were others who fared worse in that they stayed on for years, ill and fatigued they burnt themselves out, just like the aforementioned priest and blame 'the system' for their loss of faith. Shakespeare said in his play Julius Caesar that 'The evil that men do lives after them; the good, often lies interred within their bones.' This insight must be understood as great wisdom and a warning for many a would-be missionary. The root of every problem is the underlying hold that satan has on people in this part of Africa.

If we can consider ourselves when we reflect on our own past heinous sins and the control they had over our lives, it is no wonder that the African has so much struggle over the occult forces that often saw him dedicated at birth to satan. If we in the west have problems overcoming the addiction of regular sin, then how much more so for the African who has actually to break his covenant with the devil; a covenant of dedication or baptism and juju implanting, at the hand of the witch-doctor. All this has to take place before he can actually begin to understand repentance, acceptance and grace from another living God, but from one who will bring order through Grace, instead of fear. The African is a victim of his circumstance and this has to be remembered when all seems desperation.

The continual backsliding has broken the heart of many a missionary and it is often confused with false conversion. The worker who realises that this is normal in behaviour in any individual and that only the Holy Spirit through conviction can bring such a sinner to repentance; prays to save his brother from death. (James 5:20) Above all the missionary must be fearless in his approach to the occult kingdom however the Bible is clear that before the devil can be ordered to flee, total submission to God has to be made. (James 4:7) Herein is found great wisdom. To attempt such a feat when sin is ruling in the soul means there is no walk with God, so there will be no power and danger will lurk at every step.

The CEW compound

I had great joy fellowshipping with my friends at the CEW mission. In the church, which for some time I took my mission boys for the Sunday service, there was genuine unadulterated worship of The Lord. The church building itself was a simply constructed hall which for some reason was half open. When the wind blew or when it rained services got extremely interesting. There was also an opportunity within this church to enter into a charismatic environment which I discovered I actually liked. It never ceased to amaze me that I found myself being drawn to open excessive bursts of spontaneous joy in such services, that I had never quite reached during my term of office at the Anglican Mission. I found a whole new meaning for being anointed. This mission church was run by a Korean Pastor and his wife and we became close friends. There was many an occasion that I was able to reflect with Pastor Wang on the need for constant heavy spiritual warfare against the enemy. Satan, it would seem, would launch an army of demons to attack every inch of success we had in our ministries. Mr Wang was the only Pastor in that country who actually understood my particular battle with and because of this we naturally had empathy over and above our brotherhood. We spent many a happy time at this mission and I and my boys used to accompany them on some of their mini crusades, to the nearby villages.

Although the CEW missionaries performed exactly similar roles in the field as the O.S. workers, in almost identical conditions as the Anglicans, there was one big difference in that they believed the onus was on the life of every missionary to preach the Gospel at every opportunity. I thank God for that.

Another aspect of true conversion which particularly enthralled me was the occasions at the mission church when an African announced that he was giving his life to Jesus and would forfeit all the jujus on his possession. During a particularly moving ceremony these were cut off and taken outside the church where they were publicly burnt while the congregation danced around singing suitably phrased choruses. The new brother or sister was hugged and kissed onto the path for Jesus.

It is well for the reader to understand the significance of these jujus. Many are placed on a child at birth and are only temporarily and speedily removed to looser draw strings as the owner grows up. There is absolute faith in the charm in that it would protect the wearer against all circumstances. There is also faith in the belief that the spirits of ancestors would be aggrieved should they be removed, as it was they who had arranged the original protection. In short the removal of personal jujus would be the equivalent of us Christians being tortured in order to reject Jesus Christ. Please understand there is no exaggeration over this. I once witnessed an attempt to remove some jujus from a would-be convert who at the ultimate point resisted. Unfortunately those ministering unto him went too far and tried to persuade him to cut them off. The whole scene became very fraught and to my shame and ignorance I just stood back and watched in horror. The wearer of the jujus went into unbelievable distress at the moment of removal and fought those who were dealing with him. They held him down and persisted. Upon removal he went into such despair that he howled like an animal. I had to run away and I have no idea as to what happened to him. Later, I questioned the Pastor involved and he assured me that he wanted to show the unfortunate man that nothing would happen once they had been removed. I knew the Pastor was wrong in his approach and my own subsequent dealings with such phenomenon proved this to be correct. However, on another occasion, on the ward of the Jafara hospital, I was called over to break the power of a juju, where the owner was challenging the medical staff proudly boasting that his juju prevented any penetration of the skin. He was ill and needed medication. The nurse physically could not put the drip needle into the man's arm. The important difference in how this situation was dealt with, as compared to the one before, was that the patient in this case was actually boasting of the power of the juju preventing anyone from administering medication. I knew exactly where he was from and whom he served and so I immediately grabbed a plastic syringe put a needle on and jabbed it into his arm 'in the name of Jesus.' He was horrified and after a momentary pause went berserk and it took three of us to hold him down. He finally became comatose. Whether this was due to his illness or the aftermath of the spiritual battle I cannot say. I left him where he lay as I received no further instruction, but the drip along with medication was administered without further fuss. Later on he was discharged as fit mentally and physically. In this case, a stand had to be made, otherwise the impotency of the nursing staff and the power of these Marabouts would be broadcast. Interestingly, after questioning the attendant nursing staff they were adamant that it was physically impossible for either of them to insert the needle into the patients arm. Something was preventing them. Whether their paralysis was due to psychosomatic suggestion or to actual evil power is left up to the reader. Either way it is irrelevant for the juju's hold was destroyed in one moment by Jesus. This is also what I describe as taking an 'instant leap of faith'. It is exactly under such circumstances that I developed a reputation; one for good and unfortunately one for bad.

Pastor Wang and his wife needed constant support in order to cope with the innumerable problems that arose with converts and my wife and I needed exactly the same support from them. Together we wheedled out agents, who were not only sent to disrupt the walk of the newly converted but were also sent as Pastors to accuse the evangelists. And so the work continued together until one day when Pastor Wang told me they were returning to Korea for a year of recuperation. Apparently they worked three years in the field and then took one off. This was a blow to us as we had recognised the spiritual worth of the couple. Before he left he told me that I and the boys from the mission would always be welcome at 'his' church and gave me the authority to baptise anyone that I thought fit. This was a strange and unusual authorisation; however I looked on his decision as a mark of his own respect for me and was suitably humbled. I did not know then that this decision was to play a significant part in only what I can describe as an unholy and hurtful occurrence at a later date.

My wife and I and the boys from our mission continued to attend the CEW church, however it was obvious that the control and respect engendered by Pastor Wang was not evident in the newly ordained local Pastor and soon there was constant stream of condemnatory sermons from the 'pulpit', which resulted in people drifting away. As I found no love in this man whatsoever, I finally made the sad decision to transfer all of our worship back to our own mission building. Soon after this we were to hold a baptism of one of our own inmates and at the same time three more of the boys, who I had allowed to attend Pastor Wang's church and foundation classes, expressed an immediate desire to follow their friend through the waters. All three were baptised on that glorious day. Then the fun started.

I was in the laboratory one afternoon when the aforementioned native Pastor called to ask me if I would like to attend the next meeting of the CEW council as it could be useful for future cooperation, to discuss a few things. I said I was honoured and surprised to find it was taking place that evening but I duly arrived somewhat early and was embarrassingly on hand to greet the council of around twenty or so, as they came in. I remember having great difficulty in conversing with people, who in the main appeared very sheepish and averted their eyes. Even so, I had no idea of the trouble that lay ahead. This came when after prayer the Chairperson for the occasion announced the only item on the agenda.

"We are here to discuss the unauthorised baptisms carried out by Mr Grummitt:"

I sat there stunned as a statement was read out as to my 'crime' of poaching converts from their mission. This was followed by a diatribe from the very Pastor who had seen me only hours before, having cordially invited me to the meeting on a pretext. I was literally in shock when asked what I had to say to rebuff these accusations. Having believed I was being asked to participate in some outreach programme which included my mission group, and then having found myself at a trial where I was in the dock, was incredible and little imagination is needed to understand my emotional turmoil. I asked for them to give me a moment for I did not know whether to laugh or cry. I do remember satan trying to take immediate control over my emotions by suggesting I should register disgust of the body which was a toothless and useless tiger. Instead I stood up and thanked everybody for inviting me to the meeting and explained the circumstances of my actual attendance which caused a few people to shuffle their feet and then quoted the Bible in relating an incident where other disciples had had their authority questioned. I confirmed to everyone that my authority to baptise came from God, through Pastor Wang and then asked then to pardon my impertinence as to consider whoever is baptised within my own mission was my own prerogative. What followed was more vitriol from the Pastor in question, including accusations of lying and then, one by one, successive members took in turns to describe my lack of authority, selfishness and disobedience. These hurt not so much because of the untruths spoken but in the ferocity of their venom. I stared at each in disbelief having showed the utmost courtesy to all. It was difficult to understand I was not fighting flesh and blood but principalities but it shook me to the core in disbelief. Was I dreaming or were these friends actually talking about me? I was witnessing spiritual warfare first hand and yet the Bible made sense again, because of its promises. These accusers were simply not themselves but conforming to the whiles of an evil spirit. Nevertheless, it felt as though I had stepped into a nightmare. The terrifying part of this whole saga was that each speaker in turn would get increasingly angry, confirming the spiritual battle.

I stopped the proceedings by standing up and walking to the centre of the round and requesting to speak. This was granted and I immediately went into prayer for the whole assembly asking forgiveness for what they were doing and walked out of the theatre. However, I did cry all the way home. It took me weeks to get over this attack and my mission group never went back to CEW. One good friend told me later that at a subsequent extraordinary meeting of the council, a member who had not been present at the condemnatory meeting confirmed that Pastor Wang had given me permission to baptise anyone within the mission and so it was decided no further action would be taken in the matter. There was no apology, no extended hand of friendship and I became a marked man as far as the pastor was concerned as I had removed three numbers from his baptismal count, which he and others considered a pointer to the success of ministry. I have subsequently wondered as to exactly what action they would have taken regarding the matter if I had been found 'guilty'. As it turned out this would not have mattered one jot, in view of what actually occurred later but I needed counselling myself and it came from another friend.

A member of my old church at Jafara having heard of the fracas called in to give me solace and gave some excellent counselling. The upshot was a curbing of my impetuosity as it only made people jealous of the mission's success. "Jealous," I repeated "Can this be true? After all, are we not talking about Christian brothers and sisters?" His enigmatic smile told me all I needed to know and I realised I had suffered another sound lesson in my life, however being suitably encouraged in my personal mission, I ploughed on

Established Church Mission number 2

To those who will condemn all Catholics to hell please don't read on as this will hurt badly. But, if there is a heart for Jesus then please consider the tale. To Catholics reading this book please allow me a certain licence and possible forgiveness.

The Catholic fathers to me were a tonic. Of course, most were Irish and I befriended one in particular who became an occasional combatant on what passed for tennis court. We never 'talked' religion and got on fine, but what I wanted to get out of him was to why the catholic churches were packed on a Sunday and why many locals seemed fervent Catholics if not Christians? (Should this be thought rude then let me say he knew exactly what I meant). He never proffered an answer, other than for me find out for myself, but the churches remained full of the oddest of characters, which occasionally included me, while attending mid-night mass on a Christmas or New Year's eve and then afterwards being completely baffled as to why we had thoroughly enjoyed it. The Catholic Mission was of course the oldest established in the region and believed above all in practical Christianity. Water, food and clothing were the major concerns and many a converted worker will be seen toiling in the distribution of whatever alms were in possession of the mission at that time. The Catholic mission was also the largest and was spread far and wide.

The answer to the question posed at the beginning of this section came to me via another Catholic priest who I bumped into on some up-country visit. This was in the form of a notorious character known as 'Father Crazy.' This priest was the most affable and loveable of all those I met and ran a long established mission. He was the most popular man to tread the streets of his local town. He often did this and reminded me of the 'pimpernel' as he was often found 'popping up' here and there carrying out some pastoral work he had to attend to. He was always laughing and this infectious and slightly worrying attribute when coupled with his one serious vice in life, allowed him to earn his nick-name. This vice was that of alcohol abuse and there were quite a few tales of him wending his way home or being assisted back to his meagre 'apartments', and meagre they were indeed. If the locals found him inebriated they would, without question, get him to his home. There was even a tale that he was found one morning fast asleep under a table of the only hotel in town.

To his own brothers he was truly crazy, but having been in Africa for twenty years without any leave, I am sure his hierarchy had conveniently forgotten about their aberrant priest other than to send him his monthly stipend. Did they merely consider he was quite mad and best left where he was, or was there another reason they kept him on? To the other missionaries from other denominations the opinions ranged from those of disgust, to genuine sympathy for his 'condition'. To the African he was everything. He was 'The Pastor', friend and encourager, always there to give a hand or a prayer or a few coins when needed. He was fantastic at comforting people in distress and being fluent in two tribal languages he was able to make them laugh. He told them about Jesus and asked them to accept him as he was, as Jesus had done. I asked him to tell me once, when I had plucked up the courage, as to why he drank so much. He paused for a while and hung his head in presumed shame. With a catch in his voice he answered. "Wouldn't you if you were thousands of miles away from Ireland, had no family to speak of, told that you could never have any sexual relationships with women, and most people thought you were mad due to your excessive love for your parishioners?" Just for a second, I believed him and my heart did a flutter, but when I looked up, the twinkle in his eye set me off laughing and we shared a beer together. That day I knew why the churches were full in his Catholic Mission. He was a better missionary than I would ever be.

The final two points I would like to make in this chapter is that often Missionaries appeared to be unprepared for the task that lay ahead of them and suffered unnecessarily. I do not know whose fault this is, however I will say that I did make one attempt to contact a large organisation in order to give my opinion over the inordinate number of their missionaries who were undergoing what seemed to be excessive trials. I never received a reply to my letters which led me to believe there was some prejudice to overcome. I realise I could be accused of interference, in a matter over which I have no jurisdiction, however when fellow workers are seen to suffer there will be hurt for them and questions for their sponsor. If there is a God given compassion for those around there is a natural desire to ensure every weapon is wielded in order fight the good fight. If a natural desire to see these weapons wielded in the best fashion, in order to break down a long existing stronghold, and driven by an overwhelming desire to get the job done, then there is desperation for all those who are dead in their sins, so you care about every missionary. If then a missionary organisation is contacted in order to bring home the sad the verifiable truths contained in this book in this book, to be ignored creates a great sadness at best, and perplexity at worse. What is the matter with people?

I have always wanted to tell this story in order that a would-be missionary would never be given a pair of rose coloured spectacles as part of their luggage. I wanted them to know about what exactly it was I faced in a region of the world I called the devil's anvil. I have lived in five countries that were either Islamic or Hindu or both by religion and have seen the effects of spirit worship first hand. What I saw in the six countries I frequented in West Africa did not compare with the rest of the continent, let alone any other country in the world I had visited.

It is true that each day I dedicated myself to seeking out and plundering the enemy's camp. I did willingly go where others would not and have been party to some unusual manifestations, but I ask for understanding because I was driven by a force that would take me to a head on confrontation with the devil, where there was only one choice to make; run or to stay. To stay meant that miracles had to take place to change a situation. Miracles did happen and people were brought into the Kingdom.

The final point regarding missionaries is that being the chief technician of the laboratories I knew how many missionaries sought treatment from the Jafara Clinic or Hospital and the statistics make interesting reading. Of the twenty two families in the region I knew of ten that had members hospitalised within two years of beginning mission work. Five other families had workers who had developed chronic conditions while in Africa. During the five years I was in the region I saw six people from these families repatriated, including my own. These figures simply do not compare in any way with a cross section of the unregenerate ex-patriot population, whose relative licentiousness seemed to keep them healthy. I believe that these statistics speak for themselves and should be noted by any missionary organisation. I also suggest they do not want to know.

In addition to the illnesses themselves many were accompanied by 'nervous' symptoms. In my opinion these were stress related owing to the incessant attack of the enemy and his hordes on any worker in the field. After all is satan really going to attack those who are already his? Is he not after the ones who would willingly go into his lair and plunder? Please note that even by my own unconfirmed and unscientific data, it will be noted one third of the group of the missionary families that I knew of in my district, appeared to never experience any problem in Africa. If we discard elements of the law of averages or so called 'chance', which of course does not exist for a Christian, we are still left with a good percentage of those entering the fray, but why did they alone stay healthy?

I believe those families come under the same attack that everyone else undergoes. I believe that they are able to persevere and overcome because the conditions and the environment are right for an abundance of grace. I believe if they are so in tune with the Lord they will be able to fend off every barb thrown at them by the enemy. I believe even when sick or wounded they do not show it, but continue in silent agony, knowing that God will restore their body and soul and that all is permitted for the honing of the character. I believe they simply do not give in because they are assured of the victory, knowing both the absolute certainty of their calling and the hope that is to come.

Faith is the big weapon of the Missionary.

In my family, in Africa, we suffered a setback that saw my wife hospitalised in England. We were under the same attack and even though it was hideous at times and incessant we still got it all wrong, because I was too busy to notice what was happening right under my nose. There is no blame on my wife for if I blame her for anything, then I am blaming myself, for does not God say we are one. What I do blame myself for is not being able to see the physical frailty of her leading up to this attack. She had clearly reached a point where she was suffering more than I, by merely being in Africa. With hindsight I can see exactly how I should have dealt with the situation better. My reserve troop was so battle fatigued that I was too busy to notice it. I do hope that wherever she is that she will forgive me for this. I was blinded by zeal, so my prayer is that it should never happen to another.

I did notice one other fact. In every bad situation satan had a specific way of concentrating his attack within a missionary family. He always attacked the wife first. If this proved unsuccessful, ensuring that he would get nowhere, he would then switch his attack to the children. Then and only then, did he attack the husband. This is an observation that has obvious indications that are both Biblical and practical. If satan cannot get at the head of the family, he will go for those he loves. If he cannot debilitate the wife, thereby imposing a terrific burden on the work of the husband, then he will make sure that the children are targeted. Either way his role is to make the husband impotent in his work, by burden. If a family upon arriving, finds that the husband is attacked straight away, sufficiently enough to disable their work, they need urgent support and counselling to understand and overcome the problem. They rarely got it, but were told to get on with the job in hand. I saw one man in a family develop a heart condition within three months of being in Africa. He was finally sent back to England where he suffered an exacerbation of the problem. After surgery he returned, as the family were on a three year contract. He arrived to find his wife a nervous wreck trying to cope with the workload he had left behind. He then had to curtail most of his previous activities and was finally shunted into doing less stressful work. I have no doubt, although I do not know for sure, he went home a broken man after three years. What exactly was the point of all this? If in the right place at the right time, and even though attacked and wounded, there will be a desire to continue in a fight that will open the living scripture of the new testament right before willing eyes. That is exactly what happened to me when I left the Anglican Mission to found my own, which was to be called the 'Shining Light Group,' or the S.L.G. as it became known. But how did this happen?

I was simply sitting in a chair in the front room of my bungalow meditating on matters with the Lord and a voice said to me "You will open a mission for Muslim boys."

Within a week I had opened it.

Chapter 6: The Compound

During the previous few weeks before I was told to open the mission, I had been trudging about the streets of Jafara and neighbouring Kalunda and had met a number of waifs and strays and persuaded them to attend a Sunday afternoon 'seminar', I held in one of the local shops. This took place when most of the sensible members of the population were enjoying a siesta.

At the end of the first week, wherein I had been told to start up the mission, I set off for my usual Sunday seminar. On one particular day I went to the shop to await the arrivals, who soon filled up the available floor space and after buying drinks and sweets all round, I expounded on the virtues of knowing who God really was and the meaning of life, all the while leading up to the main thrust of proving that man is totally incapable of saving himself from his sins. On that afternoon a heated debate with the shop keeper developed, who was advocating the scales of justice for those who died, where good works, if weighing more than bad, enabled the devotee to enter Paradise. On enquiry I discovered that he was the local Imam of that area. Surprised at his reason for allowing me to continue witnessing in his shop, I asked him to tell the people the reason why his own works were so good that he should get into Heaven. He attempted this feat, much to the derision of those around, who obviously knew him very well, which was compounded by his subsequent behaviour. Directing his anger at me, I learned that he only tolerated my talks because he was going to ask me for money to extend his shop for use as a Koranic school. As I was considered a man of religion, I was the best bet around for a soft touch. After my refusal we were all thrown out of his establishment.

There we all were, in the dust and the torpid atmosphere. I climbed into the Peugeot and enquired of any who might require lifts. No-one did, but two sheepish characters hung onto the door handle to explain to me that the small bundles of rubbish thrown out of the shops were in fact their worldly possessions. They were the Imam's students and now had gone with the wind of change, which was me, and politely enquired as to what I was going to do about it all. I said I was sorry and sought the whereabouts of their families, only to be told they were both rejected orphans. They were discarded by the remaining relatives hopefully to learn something about God, before becoming proficient in the trade hustling and stealing. The latter usually preceded a life of petty crime, deceit and deviousness, which sadly was the normal outlook for orphans. I told them about what The Lord wanted me to do and to my astonishment they said that if I wanted a compound for the mission there was one nearby. One of them was even acting as a care-taker for the owner so it would be all right to show me around. Sure enough the compound was exactly what I pictured in my mind's eye and I made a note of the name of the owner and his telephone number. I told them to insist they stay at the place overnight or any potential deal would be off. There was no problem with this because if a white man requested tenancy it was the equivalent of a heaven sent gift.

The place consisted of one large building which was divided into one separate bedroom, one toilet/ bathroom, and two other dormitory like rooms adjacent to a store area. There was also quite a large kitchen garden. All was brand new and in a state which would be immediately condemned as unfit for habitation back in Britain. It was perfect.

Having negotiated, to get the rent down to a reasonably extortionate level, and having given the Landlord just sufficient information concerning the use of the compound, in order to close the deal and leave my conscience clear, we signed a contract with a proviso that all the unfinished work would be put right. In finished state the building resembled the aftermath of a successful mortar attack. This included gaping plaster holes in walls and missing pins in the roof, exposed wires that would have to be sealed off, non-existent electrical power and an indescribable toilet, bath, etc. He smilingly agreed to put everything right and never did, which in effect ensured he would never come near the place for fear of remonstration or retribution; perfect! His dishonesty was exactly what I counted on, in securing the covert activities of the compound. We put everything right for him.

I had my first two boys for the mission and the *Shining Light Group* was born. Both boys wanted to give their lives to Jesus, but mindful of the good fortune that had come their way in such a short time, I told them this would only happen after understanding was revealed to them by God himself. They were both eventually baptised. I realise that this might leave me open to criticism but I argued to myself if God was winkling out these boys for salvation would he not like them to get some grounding first? He would not remove life before it had started. I know I might offend OSAS (once saved always saved) missionaries by insisting on a clear realisation of what baptism means for those who wish to partake, but I had already been subjected to crusades involving 'hundreds' of conversions in one night, only to see the converts the next day outside the bars and brothels of the locality. That is after the sweeping crusader had left to go back to Britain or America with tales of victory. We lived in the place and we knew better. Besides does not The Bible refer to a change of heart, and a change of character regarding conversion or 'salvation?' It really does amaze me to hear of these hundreds and sometimes even thousands of conversions in one night of crusade. Can the claimants not see that if they devoted their annual holidays to these crusades they could deal with an entire continent within a year, thereby saving us all a lot of work and we could all go home once the requisite number was reached. Is this too cynical? Well let me tell a story about a week long crusade to Africa, I was instrumental in organising, by a large American church group. They contacted my Bishop who kindly passed the sentence onto me.

The crusade involved a team of twenty or so souls who wanted to come and deliver the word. There were preachers and musicians and soloists of differing hues who later successfully demonstrated their professional standard. On behalf of the Anglican Mission I hired the one and only football stadium in the country, all the plans were formulated and eventually the team entered the country and the day of mission arrived. For convenience we put everyone in the main stand of the football ground. There must have been less than a hundred 'whites' who occupied the left hand side and several hundred natives who occupied the remaining seats.

Prior to the start of affairs, marred only by a total power failure which was restored miraculously by The Lord after prayer on the podium in front of the stand, I had tried to dissuade the Crusaders from taking up a collection as this was a very poor country and for several reasons was not a very good idea. I was admonished. "Never fear Brother Chris," I was told in front of the administrative team. "Remember the widow's mites, for the Lord's work always requires us to give something back in return. Its good teaching and good for their souls," said their leader. It was embarrassing, especially when everyone gave me that 'smile.'

We compromised by my insistence that the leader give an explanation to the locals, of the need of 'giving' at such a ceremony, and only then I would reluctantly agree to let the collection be included in the proceedings. The Crusade went well until the time came for the offering. The bins were duly brought out and sent down the line from the left hand side to the right. When they were collected the other end there was nothing left in them. Further when the altar call was announced at the end of the programme, the whole native ensemble moved of one accord to swamp the podium. I had also warned them not to have one, particularly as they were handing out gifts.

Chatting to the natives the following day they were anxious to know when I would be organising the next 'crusade' as not only did they not have to pay to get in to hear a concert, as there was some excellent gospel music and solo performances, but people actually sent buckets of money along the line for them to help themselves. Even at the end of everything a nice man called them all down to get a high quality article of clothing. Due to the 'swamping' of the podium, the T-shirts, designated for the whole week's crusade were handed out in ten minutes in order to placate the dangerous mob who threatened to shorten the lifespan of some of the missionaries.

As for the crusaders on the third night of 'crusading', while at an up-country location, they suddenly and most unexpectedly left the country by road, to later pick up a plane that was flying to London. Presumably they went home as I never heard from them again. This fateful night was not under my jurisdiction and I never had the heart to ask the unfortunate organisers of the up-country events event what it was that that had curtailed the crusade. However, I suspect it had a lot to do with the team being asked to spend the night sleeping on boards in the village communal hut. But was this not Africa? Now I really would have liked to have been a fly on the wall when this group reported back home, no doubt of the success of their missionary venture. It's not that I'm cynical, as my heart bleeds for people such as these good souls who came out with good intentions and to teach us how to do things. To say they were out of their depth is an understatement, but in all the time I was working for the Lord in Africa, I was shocked at the level of misunderstanding, intransigence and ignorance of organisations, who sent people out to work in exacting conditions without apparent reasonable research or preparation. It may have been noticed that I was more than slightly miffed that no-one took my advice at the football stadium.

West Africa proves to be a tough learning curve for anyone who cares to visit her.

Anyway our S.L.G. compound was only a stone throw from this stadium so at least we had a good harvest field where we could embrace people with our songs and testimonies, as they passed by on their way to various sporting events.

When we finally developed some organisation the compound had one boy in charge called Lamin. His inmates were selected on my various tours around the countryside. The boys had to be homeless and rejected in some way by society, so it was no wonder that we ended up with some real nasty individuals who, at times, had to be physically ejected from the compound. Throughout the three years the S.L.G compound was open, we put up with some pretty interesting characters. These included two self-confessed murderers, four alcoholics who were wife beaters, eight convicts all of whom were punished for GBH and for good measure the whole lot took drugs in one form or another. My work was cut out for me and yet the rest of Christian society considered I was insane.

Anyone who was accepted could stay as long as he liked and as long as he attempted to fit into its micro-society. He had to learn to respect his brothers and attend the regular Bible studies and worship groups. He had to accept that he would be put on chore rosters, whether it was to look for work each day, or carry out some of the innumerable household jobs.

Each morning there were prayers arranged by Lamin and each evening and night I took both prayers and Bible study, accept for Wednesdays and Sundays. On Wednesday we whooped it up for The Lord by singing choruses for an hour before going onto the streets for evangelising. On Sundays we attended some other church service while holding one for ourselves in our compound at an alternative time in the day. The services were full of praise and very noisy, simply because the West African really likes to enjoy himself in such circumstances. The double doors to the building were always thrown open, whatever the weather and people would wander in from curiosity, or just because being Christians, they felt an affinity with the spontaneity emanating from within. People wandered in and out and there with no questions asked.

When the boys were ready, and they had to be pretty ready, they were baptised. At times in the mission we were exquisitely joyful and at other times we were near to despair. The latter was either due to being robbed or more often due to the falling away of a brother into terrible sin. The African is fearfully loyal to his tribe and then kind, and in the first days it was near nigh impossible for me to extract information from them. They had a natural suspicion of anyone who wanted to help. I spent a number of interesting periods at police stations and at the main prison, seeing to the needs of members of the mission.

One character, often driving me to despair, finally got 'banged up' for an eight month stretch. On my first visit, for some reason that escapes me now, I remember giving him the full Grummitt verbal abuse, which managed to frighten both warders as well as recipient. This was rare for me, as I usual went the proverbial mile to be a Christian doormat for Jesus, however this time something snapped. He was betraying everything we stood for. My anger was probably due to his conviction for peddling 'hash', for which he received an eighteen month sentence, reduced on appeal, for I could see what would happen to the mission if he carried on the practice in the compound. After my tirade he sobbed his heart out he told me that even though a lot of the lads did some terrible things, they would never really hurt me or turn against me, meaning bringing me into disrepute. This was strangely comforting, as I felt they were mostly ungrateful and I left him to ponder his unexpected remorse. On the second visit and while sharing out goodies to the warders, to ensure that the miscreant would be at least fed enough to stay alive during his internment, he whispered in my ear asking me to smuggle in a Bible. I really got angry. "Having ignored all the teaching I have given and ending up here you now want me now to break the law and get you a Bible, so that you can sell it or worse?" He was mortified. I remember him staring at me with big sheep eyes as I left. I was full of righteous anger but felt awful after I left him.

My conscience forced me against all common sense, to smuggle a Bible in past the guards to dear Karafa, on the next visit. Either God would bless this or I would become his neighbour in the next cell. God blessed my activity, but in no small way. I could not visit him further but sent one of the boys once a week with food or goodies to ensure extension of life. Then came the day when I was told he had been 'born again' in the prison and was holding clandestine Bible studies. Circumstances prevented me ever finding out what happened to him after his release, if in fact he ever was. If indeed it did happen, I just wonder if somewhere at some Bible College there will be found this African telling a story of a crazy mission called the S.L.G.

After I put bunk beds into the rooms in the compound building, it could house fourteen boys at a time and of the eighty three inmates who passed through its portals in three years only four, in my opinion, became true disciples for The Lord. Of the remainder I cannot say, except that twenty eight were baptised and somewhere in their little hearts is a space for Jesus. I can only leave that matter to Him. Even my most trusted right hand man backslid under persecution, but who am I to judge!

Baptisms at the compound were both fun and encouragement. When we had decided that the follower was of sufficient knowledge to know what the event meant to his life and what was to happen to him after that moment of decision we set about arranging the event. The inmate invited his friends and his peers made little mementoes to remind him or her of the experience. When the day arrived I packed a picnic hamper and others brought what they could for the baptismal 'feast'. We walked a couple of miles to a spot on the beach, where we spent some time in prayer and then in exultant praise. Even now I can see the happy group wending their way up and down the dunes, much to the amusements of locals and any tourists, shouting at the top of their voices "I love the man from Galilee", until the time was ready for the immersions. I would then wade into the surf with Lamin or a visiting Pastor, ensuring I had a solid foothold before calling out the individuals. Baptism in pounding surf is an art. One has to time the immersion to coincide with a wave and be able to hold onto the recipient. If the poor individual could not swim this was even more exacting or exciting, depending on how it was viewed, as there was a possibility that the blessing could shoot the receiver straight into Head Office. On one occasion when baptising a mere slip of a sixteen year old girl, who was timid at best and downright fearful of water, being a non-swimmer, I had to literally plunge back into the sea and swim with all my might to extricate her from the undertow, after a gigantic freak wave hit the shore as she was going under. We literally 'saved' her that day but in all seriousness, she never did forgive me for telling her it would all go well at the appointed time. Although she was not part of the mission I rarely saw her again over the years, which was sad. She did not want to come anywhere near me.

After a baptism we hugged and kissed the baptised to make them feel very special and then sat around in steaming clothes, shivering and chatting and devoured our feast of sandwiches, fruits and sorrel drink. They were and are very happy memories.

I did experiment with having some girls at the compound, but even though I took the strictest precautions the results were disastrous and the idea had to be abandoned. This had nothing to do with illicit sex, which was rampant in the society anyway and available for virtually anybody, but more due to the situation creating male jealousy, favouritism and other related problems. Mama, our married cook, acted as Matron and chaperone. But it was a failure. Mama was the wife of one of the group and together with her husband they looked after a small grocery shop that we opened. This shop experiment also failed due to the fact that I never had enough money to stock it sufficiently. Anyway Mama used to cook the daily meal always on an open fire in the garden of the compound. When it rained this would take place under the porch of the front door. The daily meal consisted of rice with fish and vegetables. The vegetables would come from the compound garden where we used to grow sweet potato, maize, aubergine, peas, beans and spinach. We also produced sorrel for a local thirst quenching drink, which I really liked.

The meal for the day would be eaten from one enormous dish placed on a mat in the centre of the main room. After the Grace everyone would squat on their haunches and would eat with one hand, rolling up the rice and fish, as a ball to pop into the mouth. The meal was eaten in silence. Vegetables were left till late into the meal when they were 'shared'. Everything was washed down with water. It was very touching to observe the residents at meal times. They were always courteous, friendly and pushing their brother forward to eat. This would happen even when I knew a person to be famished and I never failed to marvel over these inbred acts of amazing kindness over food. The boys ate one other meal during the day at breakfast, consisting of bread and tea. If the money ran out for food there was no problem as one simply ate when there was food to eat. If they had to wait three days, so be it.

I have to explain how the mission was financed. Being entirely run by The Lord he had to provide everything. I put in all our family savings in and it took most of the spare cash that I earned while being in Africa. Needless to say the mission required extra funding and this came via the help of my mother, who rounded up donations in England and from one particular dear benefactor, who was a marvellous friend to us all.

We scraped through.

As I have said there was always a minimum of fourteen to feed and clothe. Then there was the rent and electricity and water to pay for as well as the constant need for firewood, always lacking in the country and consequently expensive. In addition there were the personal needs of the boys, two of which we kept at school. Every now and again one of them would get a job however they were never in employment long enough due to a variety of reasons and what they did earn did not subsidise the mission by much. When the boys went without, we also did the same in my family. This put a great strain on our marriage, as my wife found it so difficult to cope with the constant drain of resources and energy, yet through it all I knew that somehow we were doing the Lord's work

There was one particular problem which caused more anxiety to my wife, the extent of which I never realised at the time and which was also one of the most common problems facing missionaries. This was the lack of privacy. Because we belonged to the Lord then the front door was metaphorically open to all and so it was with our bungalow. In Western Africa this will mean there is a constant stream of people calling at all times and for a variety of reasons. These may range from someone wanting to sit and chat, or to need some counselling, to those requiring food or a chance to steal something from the house. Most callers ultimately would ask for money or at least for me to intervene in a problem over money.

We were burgled four times in five years and the only time I showed my disgust (for just one day) was when my entire camera equipment disappeared. This included all my reels of exposed film of beautiful birds, which I was hoping to publish.

This event took place as I went to the kitchen at the rear of the bungalow to get someone a drink of water. It was stolen by someone who knew me and they, with their colleagues, performed the feat in a professional manner in seconds. I had to learn the hard way that everything I owned belonged to Him. I only hope that a good price was fetched on the black market for the equipment and that the money was used to feed some families, instead of being used on drugs or alcohol.

Money was stolen off my person four times during my stay, during which I was mugged twice. Once, unfortunately while carrying a considerable amount. I will also tell a story when during a visit to the inner depths of a local market I had prevented a gang from robbing me. When I had the main culprit cornered I gave him a good dose of the requirements of Jesus in his life. Eventually I let the whole gang go after a suitably tongue-bashing along with an invitation to call at the mission. I re-joined my shocked family who were some 5 metres away. My wife was shaking and distraught.

"Did you not notice the knife at your stomach?" She was crying. "What did you say to them to make them run off? I really thought you were going to die." I mumbled something about having it all under control but I had no idea about the knife. Thank you God!

There were some very hard times, for us all, especially for my wife, but as seen in the next chapter some incredibly good times which made everything worthwhile, at least for me. There is, however, one story of theft which is above all others. I am not proud as to how I resolved the matter but the incident taught me something about myself and taught a few locals a thing or two. Normally women cannot abide seeing an animal in distress and I realised that Africa was probably the worst place to bring a wife who did. We had to witness many a harrowing scene and I always carried some Nembutal and syringes in my vehicle in order to put many an injured or sick animal out of its misery. One of the darkest sides to our African experience was to watch the systematic torturing of animals. For the West African life was cheap even for humans and death a common experience. To them great suffering was also a reality, so where in all this was there a need of compassion for animals? It is a different world, a different life and it had to be tolerated otherwise it would drive a foreigner to despair. It did drive my wife to despair on occasions. The occasion of this tale is somewhat different. She had rescued a handsome drake from the 'vegetable man', who called twice a week to sell us something to us that we never needed. I always told him we grew our own vegetables, and he always stood his ground, so we always ended up buying something. Apparently on this day, tightly trussed in his basket, was a bedraggled grey/black duck which due to dehydration was near to expiring.

"Pretty good chop chop." said the man to my wife. "Over my dead body." said wife who greeted me on return from the lab with the news that we had a cowering Drake hiding in one of our hedges, who would not eat and steadfastly refused to move. I think I made my usual comment regarding such acquisitions which always sounds similar to, "Do I need this, today?" and went off to make friends with the beast. Having enticed him out from his place in the hedge he promptly took up residence on our veranda, which meant I had to dispose of a remarkable amount of faecal mess every day. Anyway, when cleaned up Jeremiah turned out to be a handsome pure white drake, who later on when we presented him with a nice corral with pond and a Jemima, ended up with seventeen offspring. Before all that happened and when we were keeping him on the veranda, he was stolen one night. Somehow his benefactor, who had developed a particular friendship with Jeremiah, had sensed the tragedy and woke me early. Sure enough I found that he had gone and during the course of my searching I came across the night-watchman for the compound, who also appeared to be going through the motions of searching for something himself. I do not know whether he just grinned at me once too often that morning, or I was given some insight, or it had something to do with me blowing a fuse (for we had been burgled recently) but in pouring rain I stopped him and just stared into his face. Slightly unnerved he stopped grinning and stammered that he had been looking for the beast but could not find it. As I had not even enquired about it, his own goose was cooked! He was very sorry and that duck must be already gone. "Very nice 'chop chop,'" was repeated to me again, which made something inside me erupt. I informed him that if Jeremiah was very nice 'chop chop,' then he would be very nice 'chop chop' if the animal was not returned. I had had enough of this lousy country and all the people who wanted to steal off me and did not care whether he was even remotely responsible for the ducks disappearance or not. I had decided that I would make him so responsible and that he would be crying out for mercy before I would have to leave the country. His eyes grew huge and he began wailing and cried out how could I the big white magic man do this if I was from God? As he ran off I felt sick and went in doors to ponder at what on earth had taken hold of me and in relating the story of what I had done to my wife, we both were suitably repentant; my remorse for the level I had sunk to in an attempt to ease my general frustrations. Was it time to go home?

Twenty minutes later a bowing and scraping watchman informed me that Jeremiah had been found under a bush and was back on the veranda. So, there was no need to kill him; the watchman that is. I was so relieved, but before I could thank him he had scuttled out of my sight and forever gave me a wide berth after this episode. He was a wise man. Although appalled at my behaviour, I noticed that when I moved around and about that day, whether this was in the laboratory, the hospital or in the streets of Jafara, a lot of people were smiling and nodding and giving me a knowing look. A local told me that the bush telegraph confirmed me to be a man with hidden depths in wisdom and one that would reap terrible revenge on his enemies. Demba eyed me suspiciously. I was no longer a door mat, my standing had gone up. Horrified, I consoled myself that at least my wife had Jeremiah back with our seven cats and two tortoises.

The Wednesday night evangelising was the highlight of the week. When the group was weak in faith and knowledge we all went out together but as some matured they were sent out in strict biblical fashion, two by two, while I sat in the mission and prayed and waited for the results. People would then drift in and I used to talk about the necessity of having Jesus in their lives until the exhausted boys straggled back. The evening would end up with prayer and encouragement for those who had heard the word, before they drifted home. Often we finished really late on a Wednesday and in total darkness when the power was regularly cut. Somehow the darkness seemed to make words more poignant and penetrating, as there were no distractions. When we went out together we just walked and walked, in and out of the shanties, stopping here and there just to sing a few choruses and/or preach the word. I was in no danger of the expatriate population observing my peculiar antics as no-one would have dared to set foot in these places, however because I did such a thing, I made enemies.

A ground swell of resentment was building up between other church organisations and the S.L.G, entirely due to jealousy and cowardice. It is a sad fact that if something different is attempted, even though it is entirely Biblical, if signs and wonders follow, then the whole world will either be jealous, or will question your motives. It was seen in the Sanhedrin in the time of Jesus, The S.L.G witnessed it in Africa and even today I notice there is no difference in Britain.

During our 'walk-about' we would be invited into many a household. There was always someone who wanted healing from a variety of small complaints. There was always someone who was possessed in some way and there was always dark, dark evil to combat. We stepped out in faith every time and on every occasion. Any individual, who wanted prayer, was prayed for. The only insistence was the fact that we were going to pray in the name of Jesus Christ the Son of God. If the recipient agreed there was no objection. If he disagreed then I politely moved the group on down the road. There was never any compromise in what was done and reputation and notoriety was built steadily.

I learned early on to recognise demon possession partly from the short term history of the individual and secondly in knowing, at times, exactly who I was talking to, in that person. It sounds unbelievable but I don't recall a single failure in calling out these demons. Occasionally the release was quite traumatic and frightening, but the demons were all subject to the power of the Holy Spirit and the name of Jesus and as much as we expected them to come out, so did the local population, who although often terrified accepted events with the ease of receiving anything else around them. Everything in Africa was spiritual; good or bad.

We were living in a spirit world where manifestations were common place. Marabouts held sway over the lives of people and when a 'White magic' character came around purporting that he received his powers direct from God, why should they not believe him? Faith works miracles for God and also unfortunately for the devil. The question is does the populace believe this? In West Africa everyone believed anything was possible, however in Britain today I know very few believe in anything at all, which is the reason why many a church, finding itself devoid of the power of the Holy Spirit, is useless to those around them.

The second important explanation concerns me. Having had a 'Damascus road' anointing, having thrust myself into the Bible, having gone to my 'Nineveh', having put myself through Bible college, I had presumed this was all a natural state of affairs while growing in knowledge of the Lord. There was simply no question as to whether one should put these powers into practice as I had understood them to be the commands of Jesus; which was confirmed every time I opened my Bible. I was too busy to notice whether others were employing these gifts in their missionary work, or not, and one day it came as one of the biggest shocks in my life to discover that out of all of the missionaries in the evangelical groups working in that part of the world, only a handful understood the workings of the S.L.G. The remainder were building up a defence against the work of our mission and resentment against me. I could not believe it.

There was another problem in that I would 'heal' Muslims. What a crime to be accused of! I shall give a typical example in mitigation. Once, I was approached when I was talking to a group of people on the laboratory compound about the healing powers of God through the name of Jesus. A lady who knew me well, presented herself limping on a crutch, with what looked like a nasty swollen ankle. She immediately told everyone that she had come to be healed 'by me'. I knew her to be a practising Muslim and told her and the group that only Jesus would ensure this woman's healing, if it be in His will to do so. It seemed like a challenge and I was being set up, however I was used to these and usually any agents of satan ran away before the confrontation. In this case however it was different. She announced to the group that she knew that this man's God healed people and she went on to say that she had actually witnessed such an event. Somewhat amused at what I thought was a new approach, I again asked her if she required healing in the name of Jesus, and she replied that she did. I again questioned her motives but she was insistent, I prayed. There was an immediate healing and she ran backwards and forwards with glee to the astonishment of the crowd and me. "Sister," I cried, "now give your life to Jesus". She refused point blankly. Although very grateful to Jesus she postulated as to what was to happen to her if her husband found out? Would she be happy to get away with a severe beating? Where would she go if she had no family or friends? Who would feed her? The crowd mumbled their approval at the healing as I stood there speechless. I did not know what to say then and still would not know what to say should I experience this occurrence again. Someone in the crowd shouted "Be happy Mr Grummitt you have healed her." and the group dispersed slowly, leaving me bemused. "Lord what on earth was that all about?" After meditation it became obvious to me that we should never presume in any situation, just step out and do it and move on. We do not have to reason why and I still have no idea what that was about. Jesus would not ask for credentials. If this were the case then there would never be the story of the Samaritan in the Bible and why did nine of the ten lepers not even thank him? Yet He healed them all. (Luke 11:17-19) Mine is not to reason why.

On Wednesday nights when we were out preaching the word of God, healing and releases followed as a matter of course. There were nights when nothing happened and there were nights of great joy and some nights where the battle took casualties from the boys themselves. These were lads who could not distinguish between good and evil because of their generalised fear of the occult. Most of the boys were in constant turmoil. Because of their background I observed that there was a tremendous inner battle far beyond anything seeming to occur in Britain. The capacity for the West African in that part of the world to do evil never ceased to surprise me and would turn most western stomachs, who are used to an extremely comfortable 'moth-balled' type of existence. Although, I have to add that television does much to bring the horror of African genocides into the lives of most people in Britain, but when it is seen what man can do to man first hand it will never be forgotten. This is the latent evil which, in my opinion, is born out generations of the tribes being offered to and ruled by satan and his evil spirits.

The Christian West African has an acute awareness of this Achilles heel and one of the most heart wrenching sights is to see him repenting. This could go on for some time and the despair and tears are genuine. Forgiveness is one of the most important features of missionary work and the worker will be driven to his very limits, regarding this gift. We must never presume to believe who is 'of The Lord or who is not', otherwise we might as well start with our own congregations, however there is one matter that I preached on then and will now, as it is obvious to me that the devil causes much confusion inside churches.

If the Christian believes that after conversion, that it does not matter what form life takes after the event, as he or she is entirely justified by the Cross of Christ, they are sadly mistaken. Jesus merely opens the door for that Christian but they are to enter and take up the Cross to walk a path of discipleship with him. So says the Bible. There is great misunderstanding in the Church concerning this. If people believe that justification and sanctification are given as prizes on top of the grace of God, at the time conversion, then they will often slide back into the world and continue with habitual sin. They are not only in the greatest of danger that James tells about in his epistle (5:19-20), but at the very least, they will never exhibit the powers that this book witnesses to.

I want to make this as clear to the reader as I did to the boys in the mission.

The difference regarding the boys in the mission is that they wanted desperately to be good disciples, all the time, but what they had to overcome each day in picking up their individual crosses, would horrify the comfortable western Christian. Often they failed, often they repented. Often they drove me to despair when they committed a crime of passion or worse, ending up in the local or main jail, but in a way this did not matter as try as I might I just could not abandon them and little by little they all improved.

I will leave this chapter on a sad note knowing that my failing should still encourage even the most faint-hearted amongst us, but I have to tell exactly how I felt in my part of Africa and why I fell into what seemed bigotry. I want this trap to be recognised for what it is.

There were times when I was torn between my mission and family and in some extreme cases chose to put the mission before my loved ones. That was a major error and something I had to learn from. My motives, and contradictory moods of both patience and impetuosity, at times were great assets but detrimental in others. It is always seemed a question of balance. My levels of tolerance were not the same as others due to what I had been taught, witnessed and believed, I still have great difficulty in believing that other people cannot see what I consider to be the 'right way' as I am glad to say when correctly admonished I would go straight back to my Bible and ask the Lord to explain it to me. I am glad to say He always does. I often consider what man postulates but I always listen to what God says and can thoroughly recommend this method of chastisement. There is no one person, no wonderful tape, no course and no singular book, other than the Bible, that can lead any person to the truth or bring satisfaction or peace. Even today I tell people I would welcome any form of criticism, as long as it is supported by the word in the book.

The resentment harboured by other church groups against the activities of the S.L.G did not worry me for a long time but when I noticed this attitude taking effect on us I became increasingly agitated, especially when the S.L.G began to be shunned at Christian gatherings. I then fell into the same trap that my critics were in and started resenting them. I even thought for a while that we alone held the truth, and they could not as seen by their attitude, which saddens me even now as I read my own words. I thank God that He was steering me through all this. However, there was one dark authority that was taking a serious interest in the mission; collecting evidence for the future, and this authority was as old and as evil as time immemorial and was to bring me undue hardship.

Chapter 7: Miracles

As it can been seen from previous chapters, miracles were relatively common in our lives and in that of the lives of the members of the S.L.G and so it is important to give a definition of exactly what this constitutes. My definition has been evolved out of the 'events' connected with my ministry as a born again believer. All the miracles spoken about in this book, and indeed the numerous others that have followed, fall strictly into this category.

'It is an act of grace by God, often given through man, whereby a situation, which may be spiritual or temporal, is altered in an inexplicable way, often instantly and visibly for the benefit of mankind and always for the Glory of God.'

I am concerned over the debate that seems to be a preoccupation with Christian groups over the years. While one group believes that these miracles were limited to the first century in order to get the Church going, another group has to convene a whole series of committees and the collection of data over several months in order to establish if a single 'incident' ever took place. (I find this incredible) Another group believes that such gifts for the working of miracles is given to a few suitably chosen individuals while yet another believes the power is given to every 'born again' individual. Is it any wonder that the Church sometimes staggers under the weight of its self-created burdens, when everything is clear as crystal in the Bible?

In the S.L.G no-one, least of all me, gave the slightest consideration as to any argument, or to decision who was worthy or not to when a course of action was carried out, or to whether an individual was a sinner or from a another faith. We all just got on with the job. I had never really been a born again believer in Britain, before I was plunged into work in Africa and I thank God that I was never challenged by philosophical or theological argument which, in my opinion, creates impotency when it comes to carrying out the Grand Commission. I thank God that I was so ignorant that I presumed that 'miracle working' was natural. It is true that after reading my Bible I discovered that the Commission applied to me, and fell to my knees at differing times, to ask for the gifts of the Spirit; in particular that of faith, healing and discernment. I considered this the right and duty of all Christians to do so. Is this the sole reason I was given them? Yet again I ask for leniency if incredulity is experienced. I did not then, nor since, act in arrogance but only in truth. After I left the Anglican mission I did but read what was contained in the Bible and acted upon it; I did but ask and was given and I did go forth and prisoners were set free. I did not report to any higher authority other than to God. There were no hindrances, no impediments and especially no loyalty to a denomination, catechism or single man upon this earth. Is this the reason why it all happened and if so, is this the reason why little is seen in own back yard? I am not pretending to know the answers, for that would be far too presumptuous but I have the courage to ask the question. Do these miracles continue in my life today? They do, but outside a close circle of friends I am forced to keep my own counsel due to persecution. Very few believe and even less want to know.

I have just read the section in my own Bible Dictionary about miracles and I am yet again appalled about the argument, legal clap-trap and ignorance covering the page before me. It is obvious that it is written by a person who has never been subjected to such a manifestation in their lives. In short it is nothing but confusing. A miracle is nothing but wonderful and astounding to all who witness. All I know about is what happened when we called on the name of The Lord, through the intercession of Jesus, and nothing in this world could ever be needed as an explanation or indeed given as a substitute for the signs and wonders the S.L.G witnessed. I do not have to make any excuses or begin to justify anything that took place but will gladly let the Holy Spirit talk to a reader, throughout the pages of this book.

Let us now turn to the Bible and see what The Lord Jesus said about us being able to use power, in order to be instrumental in miracle working. I hope this should clear up a few grey areas for those who, as yet, have only experienced confusion regarding the matter of miracle working. Hopefully this next little passage will show us as to whom it was that Jesus expected to take up the mantle of such works as a chore, and I will discuss what might happen if we choose to disobey his teachings.

"But when the Holy Spirit comes upon you, you will be filled with power, and you will be witnesses for me in Jerusalem, in all Judaea and Samaria, and to the ends of the earth." .
(Acts 1:8)

It can be seen that the power to witness comes from the Holy Spirit. Jesus was talking to the Apostles but note that he says that His word would be preached to the ends of the earth. He gives no time span and certainly the disciples of that day were totally unaware of aborigines, for example, so the commission was not laid down just for the twelve but for the church of the future; for it to take up witnessing to the very end.

"Believers will be given the power to perform miracles: they will drive out demons in my name; they will speak in strange tongues."
(Mark 16:17)

Jesus was adamant. He expected that workers would go out and perform the miracles that he himself had performed, through the power given Him by the Father. Does he talk of his eleven or of Apostles or of Disciples? No he does not. He speaks of 'Believers,' thereby passing on the power to all those in Christ who wish to exercise it

"If they pick up snakes or drink any poison, they will not be harmed; they will place their hands on sick people, who will get well."
(Mark: 16-18)

Again who was this 'they' to whom Jesus was referring to? Again it was the Believers, including those throughout the age. The Commission is clear. If Jesus had meant simply the Apostles He would have said "You" will go or, "You will pick up," etc. If His words do not refer to miraculous events then I cannot begin to suggest what they constitute. I do believe there is no argument to the fact that Jesus expects every born again believer to get out into the fray and drive out demons and place hands on sick people. There is no question of doing this to everyone in the street however there are simple ways that a Christian can step out in faith. For example, should a friend declare a headache then simply place hands on them and pray. Why ever not? What have we to lose?

If there is awareness of a possession, or even a suspicion then quietly tell that demon to come out in the name of Jesus. What has a Christian to lose but their faith! This is the reason we do not want to exercise it, just in case something dents our weak belief. I only pray with or for people when I am led to do so by the Lord, directed either by word or circumstance, either to intercede for them or for myself. If demon possession is suspected, then usually a brief conversation with that person will determine whether this is so or otherwise. What happens then is up to The Holy Spirit and not for the Christian to worry about however, if we consistently shrink back from these situations, then nothing at all will happen in our Christian walk and then what fruit will we bear? When did we last place hands on anyone? I know for the majority this will be never, yet does not He command this? If this is so then I ask what exactly is understood as the Commission issued by the one we purport to follow?

Jesus said:

"Whoever loves me will obey my teaching. My Father will love them, and will come to them and make our home with them. Anyone who does not love me will not obey my teaching."
(John 14: 23)

So it is very clear that if the disciple obeys the teachings of Jesus, that is to go forth and witnesses the Gospel to the ends of the earth, drive out demons and lay hands on the sick, the Father will come and make a home with him, via The Holy Spirit, in the presence of Jesus. In other words all the heavenly powers will be at the disciple's disposal. If the believer shuns away from these clear instructions from Jesus, excusing themselves by their own 'fleshy' inability, or by considerations that others are better equipped for ministry, then God will not make a home with him and there will be no power. There are specific warnings from Jesus as to the commission of discipleship and with regard to the penalties if these warnings go unheeded. Many erroneously believe that these warnings are for the unsaved. They are not.

Jesus said:

"I am the vine and you are the branches. If you remain in me and I in you, you will bear much fruit; apart from me you can do nothing. If you do not remain in me, you are like a branch that is thrown away and withers; such branches are picked up, thrown into the fire and burned. If you remain in me and my words remain in you, ask whatever you wish, and it will be given you. This is to my Father's glory, that you bear much fruit, showing yourselves to be my disciples."
(John 15: 5-8)

I challenge the reader understand that these are the words of Jesus and that he is not talking to the unregenerate but to his Disciples. Nothing unsaved or dirty can possibly be grafted into Jesus, The Vine. Secondly he warns them that they (the saved?) can wither and fall off the vine. This is done simply by ignoring his commands and teachings. He specifically tells his followers that if they love Him they will keep them. Ergo, if they don't keep his commandments, He is saying they do not love him and will wither and die.

Again, it truly amazes me regarding the number of Christians who justify their worldly acts and their continuing sin, due to the 'justification of the Cross'. In other words they believe once 'saved' they do not have to evangelise, teach, drive out, lay hands on, read their Bible, pray, meet together regularly etc. etc., in order to get into Heaven. It is true that none of those things will get a person into heaven, but the Bible says that you can recognise a person who is going to heaven by how they carry out the commands of Jesus. Conversely, those who insist they are saved forever believe it is nice to do these things, but if they have missed church for several weeks, can't find their Bibles and regularly take in an inordinate amount of alcohol or 'pot', while looking at filthy things on their computer they are still loved by Jesus and justified by His shed blood. Jesus says exactly the opposite. *"If you love me you will keep my commandments."* But they cannot afford the keep them and when these Christians do get together, are seen praying up a storm for signs and wonders to happen and are terribly disappointed when nothing happens. They also consistently prophesy there will be a revival. I believe this is interminably trotted out because the individuals want to believe that it will cleanse them and they will sweep into communion with God.

When nothing happens faith suffers.

Finally let us note what Jesus says about the believer who falls away, whose faith withers in proportion to his steady neglect of God. Jesus says he will be picked up and thrown into the fire. I stress again, the author of this book does not put this belief forward but The Lord Jesus Christ simply makes it a statement, however let us grab some comfort at this point.

Jesus said:

"My sheep listen to my voice; I know them and they follow me. I give them eternal life and they shall never die. No one can snatch them away from me."
(John 10: 27-28)

This is a heart wrenching statement by someone who loves us beyond all our imagination. I simply ask, please be a believer who listens to all Jesus says, and not one of those who only read selected sayings by Him. Do all this and eternal life is promised. Jesus's sheep are the fold who both listen to Him, carry out His instructions and undeterred put on the armour of God. It is to them who Jesus is giving His comfort to. He is saying no matter what is thrown at the missionary, no matter what the hardships are, no matter how the enemy persists, He knows His sheep and their works and they will never be taken away from Him.

Imagine this same comfort being given to those who are justifying their disobedience to a Godly walk? I suggest behaviour like this make a total mockery of Christ's death, by the perpetrators, who are saying to God that even though it is clear that there are a number of instructions given by Jesus, the mere fact that He died on the cross has absolved them from obeying the commands. Is this not a perversion of the truth? Just in case there is still doubt clouding the mind, scriptures in Hebrews will eradicate this but there is considerable trouble for those who do not want to believe and ignore such teaching rarely. It has to be remembered the writer is talking to the converted not to Jews or to heathens, and it is clear instructions as to what happens to those who try God's patience. This is after the receipt of Jesus into their hearts. The writer talks about born-again believers.

'It is impossible for those who have been enlightened, who have tasted the heavenly gift, who have shared in the Holy Spirit, who have tasted the goodness of the word of God and the powers of the coming age, if they fall away, to be brought back to repentance, because to their loss they are crucifying the Son of God all over again and subjecting Him to public disgrace.' (Hebrews 6:4-6)

And *'How much more severely do you think a man deserves to be punished who has trampled underfoot, who has treated as an unholy thing the blood of the covenant that sanctified him, and who has insulted the Spirit of grace.'*
(Hebrews 10:29)

If everything I am writing about is 'foreign' to a reader, and if a believer and there is a wish to exercise your right to go as Jesus commanded, it is certain as many mistakes as I made in the beginning will follow. However, if the commission burns within, with a wish to be guided by the Holy Spirit, then He will not let any flounder for long and a new missionary will become proficient in a very short time. After all He is our God and we belong to him and the power is His not ours. In Africa, for example, I could have gone to every bed in the hospital and laid hands on every patient. Some clergymen did exactly this to no effect. Others entered the ward and prayed for everyone at the door, apparently with the same result. However, if prayer is given to God each day to send the work necessary, then he will lead. Some days the work is hard. Some days it is light and some days it is non-existent, but what exactly do we have to worry about?

When He led me to a particular bed in Africa, then things started to happen.

If any reader who does not know the Lord Jesus, but now is burdened by to the extent where there is an inner sense of rottenness within the heart, then please read on. If, after reading this book there is a feeling of hopelessness and helplessness and an agony in the soul then please understand this is due to the Lord Jesus

Christ conviction of sins, and it is perfectly normal. This is the sense of the guilt of all the sins stored as memory that have been accumulated throughout all the years, that Jesus now, right now, wants the black curse of this horror to be lifted immediately.

Please call out to Him now and tell him how sorry you are for all the terrible things that have been done and that there is a desire to feel clean again and for Him to come into your life, soul and very being, to be with you for ever. For Jesus died on the cross in order that He would be the one and only sacrifice for our sins, so if you truly believe in your heart, these sins will be completely washed away, in order that you may be a new person. If this has happened and if you experience at the time a great sorrow as well as joy and even a feeling of tremendous power, then please know that this is also so very normal. If anything resembling this has happened to you then you must take the first steps to becoming a Disciple of Jesus and practising all the good things found mentioned in this book as being in the Bible. Please try and find a local fellowship that has two characteristics:

1) They speak of born again believers and Jesus Christ as Saviour.

2) They believe in the active power and gifts of the Holy Spirit of God.

Jesus said in Matthew 7:7, '*Seek and you will find, knock and the door will be opened to you.*'

I now ask for an open heart and mind to simply enjoy the following records of astounding miracles that took place during a five years period of service. I have picked the 'cream' of the group for there were many more and maybe at some time in the future if the Lord wishes it to be so, I will put them into another book, to include the period of time from my ministry in Africa to date, but that will only take place if He says so. I count these miracles as very special events in a season in my life, like precious gems of spirituality that are gifts before which I am humble.

I do realise that I was privileged to be used and to have been simply there at the right time. If never experienced a first-hand witness of a miracle then please ask God for a blessing. I cannot put into words the feeling of joy when it happens. It is as though, all over again, an anointing of the Spirit occurs and the feeling of 'belief' is amplified. This is nearest sense of the feeling I experienced in describing these moments.

Hospitals

There were three hospitals in the country. I was professionally connected with one and spiritually connected with two. The third, which I have referred to in this book as the Chinese Hospital, due to the fact they built it as a charitable gift, was an up country establishment that I rarely visited.

My main mission was to tend to the needs of those in the Jafara clinic hospital and when called I would go to the bed of the individual to pray over them or for their situation. Death in these hospitals wards was almost a daily occurrence and I could never lose the sense of loss for an unbeliever. It was a mystery to others as to why I mourned and got annoyed with other Christian workers who seemingly, could accept this loss with impunity.

This feeling has never been assuaged. I simply cannot know how a Bible believing Christian can feel any differently. Purposeful ignorance of Biblical warnings is inexcusable.

Jesus said

"I am the way and the truth and the life. No-one comes to the Father except through me." (John14:1-6) No-one means exactly what it says. Only a non-Christian would believe otherwise.

Abdouli's daughter

Abdouli was our gardener and as compared to others was both conscientious and hard working. He would always get to work on time and was mostly cheerful and communicative, although I often wonder how we ever managed this, as neither of us was proficient in each other's language. Still, he seemed to get on with things and even when we reached a hiatus, Isatou the maid used to give him 'what for!' The two of them got on well but she did scold him quite often, especially if she saw him sitting down. Abdouli was his own compound's spiritual leader and although he was a good Muslim was covered in jujus.

Over a couple of days Isatou had been telling my wife about the illness of Abdouli's daughter and scolding him for not bringing her in for treatment. On one particular day, after a conversation with Isatou, it became apparent the child was lethargic and semi-comatose. God rang a bell in my mind and the father was despatched to bring her in past the 'Demba', by saying he was bringing the child to me at the bungalow and he duly arrived with the five year old in his arms. One cursory glance told me that she was in a deep coma which I feared was malarial. I despatched him to the hospital with a note to get her admitted under my authority.

I joined them on the ward a few minutes later and had expected to be able to take a sample of her blood to assess the intensity of the parasitaemia, prior to administration of Quinine. When I saw her I was shocked for she had entered the final death throes, which inevitably would lead to her to asphyxia or heart failure. The doctor pulled me aside and said he had informed my gardener that the child would be dead within a few minutes.

I turned to a grinning Abdouli seated by his daughter, seemingly impassive to the events unfolding. I remember being angry as I grabbed him by the shoulders and yelled at him. She was going to die unless God intervened but I would ask Jesus to heal her. Nodding his head he said that he would pray to Allah. There being no time for debate I pushed past him and laid my hands on the little chest, and cried out to Jesus to excuse the ignorance of this man as it was my desire to have her healed as she was part of my extended family. This may be strange but that is what I said. Within seconds her heaving body became still and as we watched she opened her eyes and completely bewildered sat up in the bed. After an examination by the call doctor, and this being a hospital in Jafara, she was discharged twenty minutes later. For days Abdouli talked about the great miracle that Allah had performed but Isatou told him never to repeat that in her presence as Mr Chris's God healed the child, despite his stupidity. He did not talk to her for days.

The medical student

I have previously mentioned that visiting medical students, who were keen on specialising in tropical medicine, were seconded from all over the world. They were, at best, tolerated by the medical staff and I rarely met them professionally but often chatted to them. I did this while out walking, or at some social gathering. There was one very reserved individual who though ethnically Filipino, spoke with a perfect BBC accent. This was not surprising as I discovered he studied medicine in Oxford, his family having lived in the city for three generations. I decided he was a talented loner.

Part of my remit was to be 'on-call' for the lab every third night, which was actually a pain, until I realised I could get on with my life, for a runner was despatched to get me wherever I was needed even if a couple of miles away at the mission. While on call this night I was making a late visit to the hospital, prior to getting on with a urgent cross match, and I noticed a screen around a bed and casually asked the call doctor about the situation.

"Haven't you heard?" he said "It's the medical student from Oxford. They found him about two hours ago slumped in his room. He's in a deep coma and will probably not last the evening." I asked why this was so because he presented as a very healthy specimen.

"Suicide," was the reply. "He has taken a cocktail of drugs sufficient to kill a herd of elephants."

I will never forget those words the doctor spoke because of what unfolded. I saw the suicide note, which included a list of the drugs that were taken. The list was a taunt to the doctors for the unfortunate man was saying to them, 'There is nothing you can do about it so no attempt to resuscitate please!' In this he was correct for they did not. Some blood was taken for testing in the lab as a matter of record for the files and after spending some time gazing at this beautiful young person, of which I would have assist in his post mortem. I got on my bike and peddled over to the lab. This was Africa, but suicide was unheard of.

I started the cross match, and as the blood sample from the student had clotted I spun it down to remove the serum. I decided I might as well run the tests through my chemistry analyser, while I waited on the results of the other procedure. I was reading a book when the silence in the lab was broken by the staccato beat of the analyser's printer, as it began to churn out the results.

In my own time, I wondered over to check the figures to ascertain what was left of the student's organs. Much to my surprise the results were within normal limits, including the controls. I had no idea what I had done but my analyser was known to be eccentric on occasions, so I set everything up once more and turned my attention to the cross match. Having completed this I took the units of blood over to the ward and enquired after the student. Dr Chard just shook his head. I peddled back to the lab in order to retrieve my book, lock up and go home. As I got there I heard the analyser printing out the results of the second batch and retrieved the sheet and headed for the door. Curiosity made me look at the piece of paper. I remember a fleeting moment of anger as I saw that the results were exactly the same as before, give or take a few irrelevancies, and was just about to throw them away when a voice inside my head said. 'They are normal Chris,' Rooted to the spot I listened to this voice in my head which repeated once more. "They are normal Chris." With a whoop I was out of that lab in seconds, absentmindedly leaving the door ajar, onto my bike and peddled furiously over to the hospital. Bursting onto the ward I found the doctor and told him about the lab results. Although a Christian, I could not make him understand that the young man was going to live. He said he was finished on his shift and was going home. He must have thought I had been working too hard. I went back to my bike and got out the Bible I always carried in my pannier and took it to the student's bedside. To all appearances his condition had not altered. He lay sublimely on his pillow without any sign of life. His eyes were closed and he looked as though he was at perfect peace. I began to read the Gospel of John to him. I read it slowly and continued until I could not keep my eyes open. I then left him and peddled home and woke up my wife at around 3 a.m. to tell her that he was not going to die. "That's nice dear." she said as she struggled to comprehend, before immediately falling asleep. I spent a troubled night full of excitement. Could such thing be happening? What a stupendous miracle would this be, but why Lord?

Around 7.30 a.m. I peddled away for my daily work. Should I go over to the ward? Am doing the Lord a disservice if I have to prove to myself that he would be all right? My flesh got the better of me and headed straight for the student. His bed was just across from the main doors and as I went in I could see him eating breakfast. The doctor was there and he smiled at me. I smiled back at him and returned to the lab. During my morning coffee break I went back into the ward and grilled the student. After the pleasantries, I told him exactly what had happened and what I had done in obedience to my God. He visibly relaxed and related his tale, for when he came out of his coma he expected to be in heaven. Not our heaven but the heaven of a Buddhist! He was the only Buddhist in the country!

At first he was overjoyed that there was a reason he was not dead. But what cruel god would bring him back to face misery on this earth. He became depressed but we conversed and I asked him to tell me if he remembered anything when he was comatose. He reluctantly told me of 'seeing' a voice at the top of a pit he was in and the voice kept telling him that he should come back up. Exultant, I asked him if I could read to him what I had whispered into his ear the night before. Although suspicious he said yes. After a silent prayer I told him that it was Jesus who called him and once again, gave him passages out of the book of John.

Three days later, a happy smiling ex-student got on the plane with his new Bible, with a promise that he would follow his new Master and find a fellowship on return to Britain. I say ex-student, for the world is cruel and unrelenting for he would have to leave the University. The whole matter was hushed-up, except for those who had to know, and he would have been regarded as an abject failure by his family who may even have disowned him. I prepared him and told him to cling to that cross but never heard anything more but I know he had been given a golden key. Is not Jesus kind? As for me the job had been completed. As for the medical unit no one ever spoke about the incident again. It was as though it never happened, because it could not have happened! After all he faked it, didn't he?

The married woman

There were times when alone or with my 'boys' a call for help was given when human medicine could do nothing for a patient. Such was the case with the married woman. The aforementioned doctor said, "We can do no more for her, please see if there is anything you can do. We have tried every test and a number of treatments but I'm afraid there's some evil involved here."

We stood at the foot of her bed, confronting a wild eyed woman who was horribly thin. She was brought in suffering from malnutrition and despite the efforts of the medical staff was literally wasting away before their eyes. It did not require a Ph.D. to work out that this was the influence of occult forces resulting in probable demon possession. This was confirmed by trying to approach her. She would start up a 'thin' wail and addressed me in a guttural voice. I was sure this was not her own. Either she was possessed or schizoid. I despatched one of my boys to get her husband while we stayed by her bedside. I needed to know the history, before attempting anything. All the time she stared at me, constantly fidgeting. I ordered the lady, along with anything of filth that might be in her, to stay on the bed until it was time to go.

After about an hour the husband duly arrived. It was a relief to discover that he spoke very good English. It transpired that both he and his wife were 'Christians' and everything had been well until he had had an affair with a cousin. His wife suspecting the situation had resorted to the tribal method of sorting out matters and had consulted the local Marabout, whereupon a spell was cast. The husband did not know whether the spell was for him or his cousin but then end result was that his wife was wasting away. He had already repented for what he had done and had been accepted back by the wife, but things had gone from bad to worse as his wife's appetite had diminished and in the end in order to prevent her from dying, he had brought her into the hospital. Unfortunately his church, who had been praying for the situation, had not sent anyone around to witness the problem first hand. I told him that if he was truly repentant then God had already forgiven him. I ascertained that he genuinely wanted his wife well and recognised that there was a force present that was beyond his control.

He did agree with me that as they had not paid the witch-doctor for the spell, it was almost certain it had reverted back on his wife. I asked him to believe that

God was going to do something in all this and as He was in control we should not presume what God will do, but if she was willing to come back to Him then she will be saved. (James 5: 20) The problem was she was incommunicado so I did not know her wishes but decided I would go ahead and asked him to take his wife back to his compound and we would follow.

Our arrival caused quite a stir, especially when the other women saw the unfortunate state of the wife, who could not support herself on her feet. She was practically unconscious but reverted to a wail every time I went near her, in order to help bring her in.

I told the husband to lay her in a corner of the hut and to make her comfortable. I told him to tell everyone outside to stay away from their hut on the threat that something may befall them if they did not, and I told the my boys that no matter what happened they were to stay with me and pray to Jesus to release this woman. I told the husband to inform his wife what we were about to do, whereupon she grabbed him and set up her wailing and groaning all the while clutching at her stomach. Intermittently, within this wail, I detected a second voice jabbering away in a 'tongue.' As the distraught husband insisted that she wanted release, even though we had no confirmation from her, we pressed on. I asked him to step back.

We prayed and read scripture, I abruptly told the demon that in the name of Jesus it was to come out of her and leave both her and this place and that after he had left the woman, she would be healthy and begin to eat. She would do this because she belonged to Jesus the Christ. She writhed and swore and screamed at me but this time in English and rolled herself up in a ball. My touch seemed to make her writhe even more. The noise became tremendous and while I increased my shouting at the demon the poor lady suddenly sat up and after one long wail vomited and collapsed back on the mat. The whole process had taken about ten minutes of intense energy. There was no-one left in the hut but the wife, husband and me. The silence in the village was deafening. I am happy to say the husband stepped forward and cradled the wife in his arms, while I was rooted to the spot with emotional fatigue. After a while he looked up and smiled at me and I collapsed onto a bench. She was not dead.

Later on the wife, who was now a completely different person, drank tea with us and I stayed until the evening when, re-joined by my two boys, we all had a simple meal together. She ate heartily and chatted away none the worse, telling us of how she desperately wanted to communicate with me but the 'thing' inside her prevented it. She had wanted release and told of how every time she attempted to eat or drink a violent pain used to grip her stomach and that she had gone through agonies at the hospital when they had tried to feed her normally. She was mortified over her sin.

The postscript to the above story is that they were united as a couple and in their faith for the Lord. The trouble started over the fact that she was barren and the strain and shame of being in this condition as well as the taunts directed to the husband, had caused him to wander. He went to his cousin to see if he could conceive a child by him. This is a known practice and jealousy had almost caused the death of two people. Is there not something reminiscent of old scripture here? We ended that night by cursing the work of the Marabout, releasing the family from any obligations to him and praying for the opening of her womb. Sometime in the following year she gave birth to a girl. I am glad to say that this was one couple I did see fairly frequently and I can confirm them to be committed church-goers, years later. This miracle gave me the greatest satisfaction as an example of his love for his children; however it gave me the biggest fright of my life. I had to conquer this with His strength.

The villages:

Work in the villages brought secondary rewards utterly unforeseen. Each miracle seemed to be compounded by others as the blessings rolled on.

The old man

The story I am about to relate, rates as one of the most astonishing miracles that I have ever witnessed and the scale of grace poured out by The Lord in the act and on those who were connected with the aftermath is quite extraordinary.

One day, while beavering away in my lab, I was confronted by Lamin and his cousin Sidou who were obviously in a very agitated state. During the mostly indiscernible chatter they directed at me, I gathered that I was needed at the ward, and so with them running and me peddling, we arrived outside the building. To the side of the main door lay on the ground an old man, groaning in pain with no one else in attendance.

Sidou informed me that this was his father and the boys implored me to get him hospitalised. I went in and spoke to the duty doctor who was a man who considered me an 'enemy', because of my stand for Jesus. He told me that the old man had a massive inoperable testicular or prostatic tumour, that was badly suppurating, and as he would die soon he was not going to admit him to dirty up a bed, even if I paid. I went back out to look at the man. He was obviously very near to death as complications of malnutrition and dehydration had taken hold. He was in a great deal of pain. His tumour was ghastly.

I gave the boys some money and told them to take him to the native hospital some ten miles way and get him admitted using my name. I would join them as soon as I could after I had finished my work. Two hours later I found myself at the hospital in the capital and went searching for them. I found Lamin in a corridor who took me to the old man. He was put on a filthy mattress under a bed.

If the ward was full, second tier patients were then put under the beds of those above as normal practice. I asked the one charge nurse who was on duty as to whether he had been seen by a doctor. He asked why I was wasting my money as the man was going to die soon. I repeated the question to find out that it would be that night or the morrow. This meant probably never so I insisted that he be given urgent treatment for his pain, but the nurse simply shrugged and pulled at his teeth and, God forgive me, I really wanted to hit him. I went back to the boys and told them that he was a very old man and it was obviously his time. Through streaming tears Sidou asked was there no-one to help him through his pain. I watched the frail old body. His breathing was rapid and shallow and every now and again he would shudder as the agony railed through his body. I stared at him musing on what the quality of his life must have been over the last few weeks and reflecting on the callousness of the nurse and my impotence. I was brought abruptly back to reality by Lamin saying "Why don't we heal him Mr Chris?"

I remember staring at Lamin as he repeated the question. I felt sick and hopeless standing in that ward of death and decay and despair. I just did not know what to do; what hope to offer these boys. I must have been standing there for some time for both boys had stopped crying. Lamin had taken my arm. "Are you all right Mr Chris?" I was apprehensive.

I have no idea what galvanised me into action. I told the boys to pull the mattress out from under the bed and put it in the middle of the room. I told Lamin to kneel down and put his mouth to his uncle's ear. And repeat what I was going to say. The old man simply nodded to every question which was of the standard format for salvation.

Yes, he did require healing and yes, he knew we would ask Jesus to do this. The sign came through his clenched teeth when he told Lamin that he knew that this man's God healed people. Can he now heal this old man? We had attracted a lot of attention. The charge nurse was standing over us grinning away and telling all in the ward that the man would be dead tomorrow which provoked plenty of hoots of derision from the patients all around, some of whom had left their beds to get a better view of proceedings. The babble died down and all eyes were on me. I read some scripture and then prayed the prayer with all my heart and soul. I was actually crying the prayer, not so much for the man but for the circumstances and the utter futility of everything around me because of false religion. I finished the prayer and for a second the boys and I just stared at each other. The old man had not moved and continued slowly to be racked in his agony. I ordered the mattress pushed back under the bed and accompanied by much laughter we left the ward. I was almost angry at the boys for their foolish questions. Had we cast our pearls to see them swallowed up? How dare they put me on such a spot?

Nevertheless, I took them home in silence and dropped them off at the compound. I informed them I would pick them up at 6 a.m. the following day when I would take them in to see their relative and bade them good-night.

The following morning I discovered they had left early to go to the hospital. Upon my arrival I found them in the front garden, equally agitated as the previous day. They informed me that they had gone to the ward at dawn but found that, although the mattress was in place, not one person knew where the old man was. I put my arms around them both and asked them to be prepared as I headed off towards the mortuary. No sooner had we walked a few paces we heard shouting from behind us. We turned to see the old man half walking, half running towards us with a peculiar waddling gait. Stupefied we waited for him to approach us. He fell at my feet in salutation, got up and threw his dish-dash over his face to reveal his naked torso. The ghastly suppurating mess that had seemed to cover most of his groin the day before now seemed to have shrunk to the size of a tennis ball. He was clean and natural and bubbling over with joy. He handed me some bananas and mangoes. He kept saying Yesu! Yesu!

In the torrent of words that came out, with the boys translating, he was apparently free of pain, urinating properly and could eat and drink, but most of all kept saying Jesus healed him. I could not speak for some time. The tears just ran down my cheeks. What did he know of Jesus? Absolutely nothing, except Mr Chris had healed him, as he kept saying! I marvelled as only the Lord could have revealed that to him. He was so happy and kept bowing to me. We held an impromptu service right there in the garden courtyard and he received the first teaching of his life through the translation of Lamin. It was stressed that God and not man who heals and that I needed no thanks or glory, but Jesus did. I was only the vessel that believed (only just I'm afraid) on his behalf.

On waking in the night he realised that healing had taken place and being thirsty and ravenous he had slipped out to get something to eat while the night nurse slept at the desk. Suitably replete, (even after climbing trees!) he was returning to the hospital when he saw us. He had brought some fruits back, to offer them to me in payment. And yet there was one more miracle for the Lord to perform, as our new brother was in serious danger.

Having taken him back to the ward for discharge, we were greeted with incredulity by the patients and a tirade from the duty nurse. I waited patiently and when all had subsided I said that the old man would be discharging himself into my care, and I would pay for another days stay on the ward. The nurse mumbled something to an assistant who disappeared to bring two further male staff from the adjoining ward. I sensed danger and was told that under no circumstances was the old man to leave until he had seen the doctor and if I wanted to make trouble, then the accompanying staff would escort me out of the hospital. Yet again the momentary anger and thought of violence welled up within, but I mollified my temper, settling for a stand up row with the nurse for a few minutes. What he finally said to me chilled me to the bone. "This man is very sick Mr Grummitt, and as I told you he will probably die today." I knew immediately what they intended to do as had been healed before their eyes, by Jesus. I uttered a prayer and became aware of an immediate peace. To the consternation of the boys I told the nurse that he was right. I told the terrified Lamin to tell his equally mystified uncle that he must now go and lie on his mattress, but not to tell him anything else. They protested and I snapped the orders out with such venom that they acquiesced. I placed my hands on the old man and just looked hard into his eyes and nodded my head. He resumed his position under the bed. I thanked the nurse for his assistance and trouble, paid for the extra days stay and medication for the old man in the ward and left with my two frightened charges.

Once outside the ward I told them to be silent until we were down in the courtyard garden. They confirmed their fears for the life of their relative. Did I not know they will do this to him, to which I replied I did, but then so does God. I asked them to tell me if they considered the same God who had healed the old man so miraculously, was now so impotent to deal with this situation. They sheepishly hung their heads. We prayed and sat on the hospital steps in the dusty yard to await the outcome. About an hour later the old man came smiling along the corridor and we all got into my car and went home to their compound. This was indeed a leap of faith, yet I had no alternative.

Later, the old man told us that after cowering on his mattress under the bed for some time the same nurse who abused me brought his tiny bundle of possessions and called him out to hand it to him. The nurse promptly walked off. After a while the old man decided to get up and walk down the ward aisle. The nurse was busy at the desk but the old man felt he should keep on walking out of the ward and right out of the hospital. No one stopped him leaving or apprehended during his journey through the hospital complex. He already knew the way. Praise the Lord!

This man returned to his village and ploughed his fields and planted a crop. He had the best harvest ever and even wanted me to take a major slice of the profits! Twice a week in the company of Lamin I called on that old man and read him the Gospel and taught him about discipleship of Jesus. He was formerly a practising Muslim but had no interest in any occult practices. He was baptised one glorious day with the whole village looking on. He could not read or write, but had a retentive memory. After every visit of mine he would hold his own teaching session for his family. In the eighteen months that I knew him he brought four other members of his family came to the Lord. Two being young, intelligent and speaking excellent English would have taken the word wherever they were found in Africa. Whatever he told them was sufficient for them to give their lives. On biblical knowledge the old man was poor, but in the power of the Spirit he was a lion. The Holy Spirit took over and taught him and now the family had two Bibles in English that could be translated.

As to the question why he was not ostracised by his village, God had even arranged that protection. During the return to his compound, and after announcing he was a Christian, not one plot to oust him from the village succeeded. In fact the local Marabout could not physically enter his compound, which caused the elders to leave him alone. However, ordinary folk thronged to his compound. The chief was too frightened to stop them.

The old man is with his Saviour now. He was eighty six when the Lord chose to save him. I will see him again. Members of my own family who came out to meet him from England were always struck by his infectious charisma of love and peace. The Lord never ceased to amaze me during my stay in Africa.

Angels

There are those who wonder about angels. The Bible describes a creature not dissimilar to those who are portrayed in countless paintings and drawings, that being of a benevolent white clothed humanoid, but depicting individuals with gorgeous wings for propulsion. No renaissance artist ever seemed to question why they would ever need these, if they were not a Cherubim or Seraphim. What they definitely are to man, are ministering spirits and appear to have distinct roles and functions. I am convinced they occasionally appear as men and walk this earth. (Hebrews 13:2) I have met two and will describe the one I saw in Africa.

Just such an occasion took place in the compound, when one Wednesday night a stranger darkened our door. He literally darkened the doorway. Although I do not want to run the risk of embellishing the story, it would appear from my memory that he was very tall, around 2.0 metres. He was dressed in a single flowing garment, like a long cloak, that stretched from neck to ankle. He had finely etched features and his skin shone like polished mahogany. He certainly stopped our praise session. I welcomed him, but he would not enter the room. He merely asked in English, if we had any food and water. I replied he could eat what we had left over from our evening meal for which he thanked us. As he would not move from the doorway we put the food and water into bowls. He took both from me and without any further word departed and somehow closed the door. I then noticed he had chosen to sit down in our garden with his back to us. Throughout this no boy had moved or said anything. I noticed they were trembling, and although mystified by the stranger, I felt a great sense of peace. The boys then gathered together on one side of the hut, purposefully out of sight of the visitor and began to talk at once. They were trying to tell me through their terror that he was 'of no tribe around here,' and muttered together in their anxiety. I told them to not be so stupid, I had to admit the man was disturbing, and sadly I did not recognise him for who he was, but then was I meant to?

I told the boys that our feelings were ridiculous and that to cheer ourselves up we would sing one of our more rousing choruses. We did this and soon everyone was in the swing of things and after the 'nth' rendition it died a natural death. They all moved to the window overlooking the garden. The stranger had left, without anyone noticing. The only evidence of his visit was the presence of the two bowls left on the red earth. I brought them in and to our amazement, not a drop of water or morsel of food had been touched. As everyone found this too strange to contemplate, I closed the meeting with prayer and went home to bed a puzzled man. The answer as to exactly who this stranger was came to us on an up country trip a few weeks later.

During a previous mini-crusade to one of the northern territory villages an elderly couple, having seen the effect of salvation on their son who was a member of the S.L.G, gave their lives to Jesus and professed it in their village. They were immediately thrown out by its elders and the Chief allocated them an arid piece of land outside the village perimeter, where they could settle. The S.L.G built their new house of sun-fired clay brick within a few week ends work, with the exception of a roof. This was not a problem at that time as people often slept out of doors as it was not yet the rainy season. What was of importance was the fact that the Chief had purposely barred them from using the village well. A few Jerry cans kept them going each week when I called by to replenish stocks, but this was not the long term answer. Anyway at last the roofless building was completed and we held a dedication ceremony to which a lot of the villagers attended. The urban West African would scoff at such proceedings, but his counterpart in the village was fascinated, and so it was in this village.

The problem with the water was that there was never sufficient for them to keep an animal or to irrigate any crops. Something had to be done and only God could do it. The chief had allowed the people to visit but not take them water. He allowed their visits only because eventually the couple would die or have to move on, proving their God could not provide for them. As the summer got hotter the demand increased and I was getting irritated. One evening we made this item a subject of specific prayer in the mission.

"Lord please supply the water for the compound, for all their requirements. I cannot guarantee to do this, but you can. They also need a roof Lord and there is no way we can afford that." We prayed up a storm.

On my next trip up I was delighted to see that they had use of a well; doubly amazing as it was a completely dry area. I was dumfounded at the answer to our prayers, yet how did this happen. The enormity of this miracle became apparent when they described how it came into existence. Apparently one day a stranger called and asked them for a bowl of food and water. They did not have much but, being Africa, they shared what they had. The stranger asked if he could stay the night and in return he would dig a well for them. They told him it was useless, but as he insisted they let him do it. They slept throughout and in the morning they found a well and the stranger gone. Not more than two meters down, there was water. I could not believe it. Naturally the wonder of this event was overwhelming and naturally we wanted to know who the man was that who performed the feat. Over the obligatory meal they quietly described the same mysterious visitor who came to our door at Jafara a few weeks previously. The boys were as stunned over this visitation as much as the couple were, when we informed them of our story. We went to our knees in thanksgiving and joy.

Yet another miracle awaited me when I got back to my medical station. The Director informed me sufficient material had arrived on a boat to re-roof the stores. Also, as he had neglected to inform that this was to be done, and that I would have to supervise the whole logistics of the operation, I could dispose of the old roof as I saw fit. The couple had their roofing as there were plenty of sound sheets. Exactly one week before the rains came to the region the S.L.G fitted their roof.

Is there any further evidence needed as to why my own life is utterly dedicated to Jesus? The miracles rolled on and because every single impediment put forward by the elders of the village to 'kill off' the couple was seen to be thwarted by Jesus, their new compound had a constant stream of visitors, including their old friends. The chief simply had to accept it. God had placed a table before their enemies so that they would not be put to shame. Why are such a couple so blessed while we do not see such things in Britain? The answer is that their faith is simple, uncluttered by all the worldly entrapments of western society. They are paid up members of the first group who will enter heaven and it would do us well to take good note of this. As to what develop later I have no idea but whatever God started in all these villages will bear fruit because once He starts a work He will complete it. I never have any wish to check or even wonder because I do not have to. When I left the couple my work was done.

I cannot close this chapter without telling a couple of stories concerning confrontation with the Marabouts, the witch-doctors. This was always occurring but the two following stories give me the greatest pleasure to relate, especially as one was so full of hatred for the work of the Lord, and another involved a public death threat placed on family member. Up till then I had only be targeted with charms and fetishes attached to my bungalow, which I merely destroyed.

Marabout number 1

Once a week I used to open a medical clinic, up-country in a village called Lubbock. I did this to keep up a tradition started by an old medical worker who had found that it was too much for her to continue. Although purporting to be a Christian, this dear lady had given Lubbock money to build a mosque before she went home for retirement. Although I loved the village elders dearly, I cursed this project which was abandoned after a few weeks, seemingly for no reason. I feared the money had been 'spirited away'. If the good lady had known that this was probably going to happen then she would have allowed me to build the village a decent clinic, which would have been put to far better use.

I really loved these people in this village as I got to know them personally and they in return respected me. They respected me because people got healed. Healing at this clinic, which was a ramshackle building, was 20% medicine and the rest was placed purposefully in the Lord's domain, under their requests.

When I arrived at each allotted time in my vehicle, I unpacked my basic medicines, set up the tables and within minutes a queue had appeared outside the door. I gave each a cursory examination and separated those who were acutely ill, from the remainder who patiently waited outside, while I dealt with them first. Fevers were treated according to the season. Almost all were malarial in the wet and viral in the dry. I dispensed a great deal of aspirin, ointments, malarial prophylactics, Kaolin et Morph and the usual basic stuff, however I always asked at the end of the proceedings whether I could pray over the individual. At first no-one wanted this but one by one, through need, a few agreed and then it became a normal part of the process, because of what occurred.

The reputation started after people were brought out of comas and others were saved from the witch-doctor's medicines. I have seen people covered in indescribable muck, resembling a tar like substance, which always made the patient worse. This was countered by prayer and the practice diminished. The villagers were happy and the elders were so content that they came to pray 'over me' on several occasions while seated outside the clinic, but the village Marabout must have been seething in hatred.

Matters came to a head one day when I was called hurriedly from the clinic to a woman who was in delirium and nearly full term in her pregnancy. I presumed she had been suffering some toxaemia for some time and now was about to die from it. She was covered in the evil muck and the witch-doctor (a woman herself) had pronounced the baby dead in her uterus and the patient in a terminal condition. It took a lot for the family to call me against her wishes. Even so, I sensed no particular spiritual excitement, merely put my hands on her and prayed for patient and baby. She quieted and I told the family to make her as comfortable as possible, finished my clinic and went home. I admit I feared the worse.

At the next visit it seemed that everybody was out to greet me when I entered and I could only made slow progress to the clinic. When installed they brought me the same woman whom I prayed over. She presented with a healthy baby boy sucking at her breast. Everyone was beaming. When an African smiles, the teeth say it all. No-one was communicating but everyone wanted to just be there and be happy when I showed my obvious joy for mother and baby. They eventually dispersed, I got on with the clinic, dispensed all forms of medicine and on finishing packed up to go.

The boys were the first to notice that everyone seemed to have vanished. Nevertheless we wound our way through the village in the Rover until the track joined with what passed as the main street. I could see people inside the buildings but they would not come out. It was eerie. All of a sudden the witch-doctor jumped out in front of my vehicle which I brought to a stop as she started chanting something at us. My attendant boys 'flew' out of the back of the transport.

The apparition dressed her regalia, had a chicken in one hand and a knife in the other.

I just slowly lit my pipe as she danced around my Land Rover. Without warning and to my disgust, she whipped the head off the chicken and covered my vehicle with spatters of blood. I leapt out in order to confront her as she stop her dousing and pointed the decapitated chicken my way. Speaking in English she informed that I would find my son dead when I got home and then ran off and 'disappeared' between the huts.

This was a new development in the warfare and it shook me somewhat, so after a short prayer I got back into the Rover and drove to the outskirts of the village, where my two boys joined me a few minutes later. Suitably admonished they cowered in the back of the vehicle until I dropped them of at the compound, where they were forced to clean my vehicle in punishment for deserting me. I then slowly drove home to my Bungalow. My wife and I prayed against the curse. Stephen our son was out visiting with friends and we were tempted to go and get him, but I insisted that we act normally and stand on our faith. Stephen returned and although we kept a wary eye on him that evening, he remained happy and healthy, as he does today. The bush telegraph later confirmed the Marabout in that village, having failed in her quest was forced to pack up and leave as people knew that her powers over them were broken for ever. My son did not die and I was considered the new 'Marabout' for the village. God forbid!

When I left Africa, I did think of Lubbock now and again, which undoubtedly reverted back to its old ways after I had gone. This is as inevitable as death, so the work will go on for the needy, but when good works stop for a while it is heart-breaking. The pain of leaving people behind can only be imagined by those who have suffered much. I asked Lord to look after them and quickly send the next Tubab to look after the clinic.

Marabout number 2

As I have said before, we made the occasional foray to villages in order to stand in the centre called the Bantaba, and deliver the Gospel. Usually we arrived uninvited and after negotiating with the Chief were given permission to talk. I always carried some medicine as negotiating material. I did not see this as bribery as the items could only do some good for the people. So, it came as a very big surprise to find that one day we were approached and invited to preach the gospel in a far off village. I immediately confirmed that we would be there at the appointed hour, which caused concern with the boys for we were going across the river to the largest village in the north section. They doubted the motives of the elders. I must add that whenever confronted I had no fear. I have no answer as to why this was other than it never seemed an issue. The reason I mention this is that I experienced an awareness of the presence of God in Africa that is not the same today. I will leave it at that, but will say I have no answer as to why this is. I believe it is not that I am frightened at all, but Africa warranted some sort of special anointing.

Having chided the boys for their own anxiety their assessment of the situation proved to be correct, for upon arrival at the village, it was obvious that a confrontation had been arranged. The village was indeed large and I was led to the centre circle where I was presented to the Chief, who spoke reasonable English and to the elders who numbered about eight or so men. These men sat with a semicircle in the shadow a big Baobab tree in old arm chairs. The evidence of these, plus their fine attire, attested to the wealth of the village and to the importance of the occasion. I also noticed that that they were dressed up in their 'Friday' best and because of the extent of the organisational skills, I was probably being set up for something extraordinary. The Alkelo or chief bubbled over with enthusiasm.

"Please tell us when you want to start."

"Do you know why I am here?"

"But of course, you are going to tell us about your Jesus."

"I am going to preach to you the Gospel of Jesus Christ."

"Yes of course and afterwards we are going to test the power of your God."

I was very uneasy now. "What do you mean?"

"You will see and you may begin." He sat down in his arm chair and I mounted an upturned crate. I have to say although unnerved at the beginning when it was obvious that there was a challenge issued, I became really excited. How could I not? He would never let me be put to shame! (Romans 10:11)

"I have to warn you chief that if you challenge God then he could get very angry." The Chief translated to the others who started laughing. The chief spoke once more, with malice. "You think you are right, but we will show you the power of our religion…speak!"

His obvious malice actually calmed me by making be angry. I hope this can be understood. When really annoyed at something, all fear disappears. It was the best possible righteous anger. I began by telling the Chief that the Gospel was for everyone, whereupon he stood up clapped his hand a whole horde of people poured noisily out of the huts and formed up around us at a respectable distance. The chief silenced them and smiled at me. Everything had been well rehearsed. Now I marvelled that all this should have been arranged just for me. If only they could see me back home?

No sooner had I started talking, the chief interrupted me. Everyone was laughing. He told me to go slowly for the translator and warned me at any time the elders may want to question me. I was not further encouraged by Lamin whispering to me that the Marabouts in this village were very powerful. No matter what I said I was constantly interrupted by the Chief to be told how the Koran differed in its teaching. In return I gave a rebuff. This continued for about a quarter of an hour during which I had explained, and argued, the necessity of salvation and the fact that Jesus was the Son of God. The chief simply got more annoyed at each interjection and on the last occasion leaped to his feet and barked out an order. At this a large part of the throng encircling us fell back to reveal a magnificent Marabout in all his finest feathers who was striding towards us. I glanced at the Chief who was smiling at me. Within an instant I knew what to do. I jumped down off the crate and stretching out my hand toward the Marabout I said.

"In the name of Jesus Christ I will not permit you to interfere here."

The Marabout stopped about 10 metres away and began to jump up and down. People started murmuring, and then began shouting until there was general uproar. The Chief silenced this and called on the Marabout to come over and because he would not comply went over to him, to physically pull him into the circus. He found that he could not, for the man was incapable of going forward. Whatever he did he could not get any nearer to me. Praise the Lord!

I simply got back on my crate and started preaching which silenced the crowd. After gathering his senses the Chief told everyone to go back to their huts and one by one the elders left, until I and Lamin were the only persons standing by the Baobab. The Marabout stayed as though transfixed to his spot. I finished the Gospel and without further ado got into my vehicle and drove home. I remember a grinning Lamin sitting next to me, throwing his arms around in glee saying "Wha! Wha! Mr Chris, how you do dis ting, you mus tichme."

He kept on grinning and shaking his head all the way home. I was exultant.

The gospel had been preached. It was definitely not on the agenda of the Alkelo.

Chapter 8: The End

The end came suddenly, however it was not entirely unforeseen. I had received a warning in a dream. As I do not normally remember a single dream upon waking, I considered this a direct message from God and redoubled my efforts to bring people into the Kingdom. I preached wherever I could that the end times were coming, which incidentally I still believe are imminent, and exhorted the boys in the mission to 'get in and get out' which was our maxim. That is, to 'get into the Kingdom and get out on the road.' We now spent four nights a week out on the road evangelising and all the time I developed paranoia about the fact that time was running out. Little did I realise that the Lord was in fact indicating, that it was not specifically running out for the world, but for me in Africa.

One night I was sitting reading my Bible in the compound when three men walked into the building. As always, I greeted arrivals and asked them to sit down and have some nourishment. They declined but asked me to tell them about the S.L.G, which I did. They then asked me for some historical details and I was immediately alerted when one of them took out a notebook and told his colleague to have a look around the place. In fact both his colleagues disappeared into the other rooms. I then asked the man to tell me who he was, to be informed that they were Interior Police, and my heart sank right into my boots. They asked where the boys were and I told them, and we then waited in silence for their return. It was probably the worst two hours of my life, waiting and knowing. We sat in the evening light until the boys started to drift in.

As they did this, the officers took them to their rooms and searched their possessions and bed rolls. I thank God that not one item that could be called a weapon, except garden instruments, could be found. There were no drugs either, which I found extremely gratifying and praised the Lord for his mercy.

I only interjected once and was told to 'shut up', which confirmed we were in serious trouble. The boys sat silently along a bench against one wall and we waited until the last inmate had arrived and I informed our guests of the fact. After a pause the leader stood up and ordered all the boys to have all their possessions packed within five minutes and they were then to leave the building and stand by the outside wall. After this exercise had been completed, I was escorted out and the officer informed the boys that the S.L.G was being disbanded owing to the crimes it had committed, mostly in this building by Mr Grummitt. No-one said a word. He then gave the boys an option. They could leave immediately and get out of the district or they could stay, in which case they would be charged alongside me. Further, should they decide to go, no attempt in the future must be made to contact me. If they did they would suffer the same fate as me.

Please try and imagine my thoughts at this time.

There then followed a long pause during which there was silence until one by one the boys picked up their bundles and with just a glance at me walked off down the road. With tear filled eyes I simply said 'God be with you.' as each one shuffled by. To Lamin I whispered. "Please get help!"

They were hard young boys. They would get over it, but I wanted to drop to my knees in grief. I never saw them again and within the hour I was in a local police cell being interrogated. The detective was quite polite at first and told me that I was obviously a good man to look after African boys but there were limits as to what should be done. I told him I had done nothing wrong and if I was to be arrested then I must know what it is for. Strangely I did feel at peace, as though welcoming the confrontation. I wanted to know exactly what it was I was charged with and who had pointed the finger at me. He just kept asking me to confess my crimes.

Eventually this gentleman was joined by his buddies and things warmed up considerably. A document was produced and was shoved under my nose to sign, which I refused to do as I could hardly read it. This interrogation was kept up for a time and eventually upon my protestations they allowed me to make one telephone call. I was taken to another room and I just wondered if I dared to try for an outside line. What happened was incredible. I dialled out for the U.K and to my surprise got through to my mother in Clare, Suffolk. In the briefest possible conversation, lest I raise suspicion, I told her that I was in prison and not to worry, she was not to tell my wife but to get members of the four churches in Clare together to pray for my release. My guards realised something was amiss and bundled me back to my cell.

On the second day they informed me of my crimes. I had run a house of male prostitution from which I also peddled drugs. I was also involved in the laundering of money and stolen goods. There were a whole stream of minor misdemeanours, however incredibly, attached to the bottom of this list, was the crime of actively seducing Muslims to turn away from their faith. They saw me smile upon reading this which made them mad however they promised me that if I should just sign the document I could go home on bail. I took the list and crossed out all the crimes until I reached the last where I wrote one word after the clause; that of 'gladly'. They were so angry at this they threw me in with the 'Riffraff' which was amusing. Up till then I had been 'housed' separately. I was now was in the main cell block for minor miscreants.

On entering the stinking hole I was greeted like a long lost brother. Naturally, due to my wanderings, all the prisoners knew me and so we squatted down for a chat. On hearing of what happened to me they set up such a caterwauling that we were threatened with clubbing. I quieted them down as I set about ascertaining their own crimes. Most of them were in for petty thefts and I searched my pockets for cash, as I had surrendered nothing but my passport and found,

'Glory to God.' I had enough to pay off their fines. The police used this system of petty fining in order to bolster their income. They could not be really held to blame, as often they received no pay for the week and the urchins, like the ones who were with me, were guilty of their crimes and should pay. They were pretty annoyed however when I practically emptied the police cell.

I did have a visitor thanks to Lamin.

The Administrative officer of the laboratory had found me and after telling my captors what he thought of them and realising he would get no-where, he went out and bought me food and drink. This was welcome as there were no such niceties at these hotels. He also got me back into a private room, in fact a small store room, and he did me an enormous favour. From a whispered conversation, he arranged for some air tickets to be available for me on the plane to London the next day. He said somehow I had to get out and I nodded. When we could not talk any more he threatened the police with severe action, if my passport was not returned to me. They simply smiled at him and showed him the door. I told my colleague the good Lord would get me out if it was in His will. I'm afraid this did not warrant an encouraging response from him. He simply thought that in the first place that I was absolutely mad to do what I had done, and secondly he considered that I was downright arrogant in the extreme, to presume to come into a country, in order to change its religion. He was only doing what he could for me because I was a colleague and he was doing his job. I told him that was fair and that I would be eternally grateful. I believe the remonstration actually allayed any suspicion that we might have been in collusion, although he was not acting. He was an atheist.

Sometime early the next day I was presented with a new document of my 'crimes.' The only clause on the document was the one of subverting Muslims in their faith. I stared at the document and then asked the policemen to keep his promise of probation if I declared my guilt for the crime. He agreed and incredibly after signing handed over my passport in a miraculous way. I saw he had it in his top pocket and I looked him in the face and insisted that he should give it to me. There was a long pause. He seemed to be mystified. I uttered a prayer and repeated. "I think you should now give me my passport." He continued to look puzzled but slowly took it out of his pocket and handed to me; the only item that could curtail passage on my part. It was the last thing they would let me have.

I breathed a long sigh of relief and offered up an enormous thank you. The officer told me that until my arrangement at a magistrate's court, where I would be formally charged, I had to report nightly to the arresting station. Once charged I would be held in custody at the city prison until my trial. At least it was a place I knew well. I thanked him for his understanding signed some documents and left.

I ran home, hurriedly packed some things into a suitcase, tried to explain to my frantic maid of what had happened, got my tickets and was driven post-haste to the airport. This was hours before the flight but as I had authorisation to visit the airport, due to my job, so there was no suspicion raised upon my entry but I have to admit the wait in the airport, especially in the half hour spent in the departure lounge was fraught. I think I prayed continually, and at one time the guards came in and took someone else away. I had to remind myself who I belonged to after my heart beat returned to normal.

That very afternoon I was on a plane to London. I had gambled on the laws of natural inefficiency in this country of Africa. The Police would not have believed that I could have arranged my exit from the country within two hours of being released and the borders were probably closed to me the following day, when I was already home in the bosom of my startled family. All they had to do was telephone the airport on the day I left and if they realised I had checked in, I would have been immediately transferred to the main prison in the capital. There was a downside to all of this which filled my thoughts on the plane.

It was sad that someone had to be pushed off the plane for me, as the seats were always booked up weeks in advance and I am sorry about that situation. I am also sorry for those who were inevitably punished for my escape, especially the policeman who handed me my passport, but I have left behind my grieving for all concerned. The only comfort lies in knowing the Lord engineered my escape from Africa. This was underscored when later I discovered the very moment I was handed my passport and given my release document, coincided exactly when members of differing denominations in Clare were praying for such a happening in a church. Praise Him!

Unfortunately, I am still 'persona non grata.' In a number of African countries and cannot set foot in them, until the Lord says so. I do not know where the boys are, but the Lord scatters his church abroad for His Glory. Later I was informed that in the following weeks there were requests to have me extradited to face a long list of charges. The strange thing is I desperately wanted to go back, mostly due to a false sense of guilt and sense at failure at letting both God and the boys down, however I finally listened to good advice from my family and friends and especially from my former employers, who were highly supportive in every way. This was unexpected as I had let them down badly, however the Secretary of the governing body, who dealt with my case, turned out to be a born again Christian and was completely sympathetic to my work. He even described it as a blessing! Other government officials smoothed everything over from a diplomatic point of view.

I was also given information on the 'witnesses' arraigned against me. They were former members of the S.L.G who had been drug dealers and one was a practising homosexual. All were ejected from the S.L.G fellowship because they refused to change their associated habits and wanted to use the mission as a front. They had testified in court that I had taken hard drugs and had illicit sex with them. All had been pardoned for their crimes for turning 'states evidence' against me. I wondered what happened to them after it was obvious that I was not to come back. As to the heinous crime of subverting Muslims the list of names was long, and it was the only thing I accepted, as well as being the only truth in the matter. I marvelled at the existence of the list and its authenticity. However, what I did not realise that technically the charges of proselytising and engaging in illicit sex both carried the death penalty, which is why so much fuss was made.

The poor S.L.G had gone out just once too often and had 'converted' one too many a local to Christianity. Sadly, I also was told the established churches were very glad that the mission had gone for the S.L.G rocked the very foundation of relationships. This may sound odd but it has to be understood that established missions never actually went out of their way to convert anybody in their works, but merely look after generations of relatives of converts. To the unsaved they gave schooling, clothes, food and wells, but only rarely did they rock the boat with an actual conversion. The sad fact I have had to face was the more active the S.L.G was in evangelism; the more the relationship between the Christian fraternity and the authorities destabilised, even though they disowned us. Anyway they were glad we had gone while the authorities fumed over my escape.

The actual demise of the mission started when Lamin went back to his family village and preached the Gospel when his uncle was present. His uncle, a devout Muslim and a defender of the country's faith, also happened to be the Minister of the Interior. He never told me of this at the time but from that day the Shining Light Group was doomed.

Months after I arrived in Britain I was sent a letter, purporting to come from Lamin, and in it he said that he had recanted and was now attending a mosque. It was awful to read this letter, in his own handwriting. I hope he did not suffer too much at their hands.

Even though I am at total peace now concerning everything, this was only due to the fact that the Lord, one day, told a former colleague and friend to give me a word that I must stop fretting. Is not the Lord faithful?

Epilogue

I started this book by saying that it is a testimony of encouragement and I finish it by saying the same thing. It is an encouragement both for the believer to take a step in discipleship and for the unbeliever to get a glimpse of the power of God, in order for them to take the very first steps on a path of glory. It is an encouragement for those, who may have been Christians for years, to take that step in faith; to realise that all those uncomfortable questions that have been conveniently pushed to the back of the mind can now be answered. To realise that it is possible, no matter how discouraged we may feel, a personal relationship with Jesus is actually a reality. He then lives within. It is particularly for those who might feel that they are only the lowest in the Kingdom. Despite any disbelief, poor teaching, confusing doctrines and a general overwhelming sense of inadequacy, it is Jesus is through the Holy Spirit who will create a dynamic change in a life, should it be requested. Jesus promises that when we are weak His strength will abound. (1 Corinthians 27)

If any believe that there are specific functions in the church that are way beyond their personal capability and that by simply attending a church salvation is secured then they have faith in a lie. However, if knowledge of the Kingdom of God is acquired it will be realised that there are gifts and callings for all. Everyone has the right to a wonderful role within the Kingdom, and I mean without exception. God is no respecter of possessions, position or even person in the sense that He treats everyone the same. If He knows the number of every individual hair on our head (Luke 12:7) then he knows about every single one of his flock. He is merely asking us to become born again.

Once full of the grace of this simple gift we can ask him to take us onto glory; to note what Paul said in his writing to believers in the Corinthian church.

'Whoever does not have the Holy Spirit cannot receive the gifts that come from God's Spirit. Such a person really does not understand them; they are nonsense to him, because their value can be judged only on a spiritual basis.
(1 Corinthians 2: 14)

This is not a book about salvation. Salvation is a personal matter between God and the recipient and it is received by His grace through faith, and in no other way; when we understand we are on the path towards it. (Ephesians 2:8) This book is to point out to believers that there are certain rules for disciples in order to obtain abundant gifts of grace, in order to go out to heal the sick and drive out the enemy at every opportunity, whether for a Christian or not, thereby only bringing glory to God.

I now would like us to examine why the Lord has chosen to write this book now as an encouragement.

In modern terms there has never been a time of such traumatic upheaval in the events of the Christian Church in Britain. The enemy has attacked by allowing such a dilution of the word, that in many cases the truth has been perverted beyond all Christian belief. However, to counteract this Godly men and women have been chosen both to bring the fundamental teachings back to the truth found in the Bible. There is a continual see-sawing battle that is now reaching monumental proportions. As soon as a false prophet is raised up then God calls on a Godly person to counteract the fallacies.

Whether or not the battle is being won or lost is irrelevant to the spiritual education and joy that is open to all believers in the Gospel of Jesus Christ. If the Church appears to be in spiritual decay, then there is a need for someone to do something about it. The dedicated Christian sees these times as a wonderful opportunity to get into 'the fray' and make disciples of the people before the end, which is why such disciples realise that they are of the chosen. They are of those whom the Lord is calling to make a difference in a world that is becoming confused by the day; always remembering it is Jesus who continues to build His church, not us!

Contrary to public belief and wishful thinking, God does not bring revival when His children are disobedient; He brings judgement. The judgement will be upon the nation; a nation that has been under his protection ever since the Gospel was accepted in Britain. Are we ready for this judgement? Can we avert this judgement? Do we have to worry about it?

This book is designed to alert the Christian to a personal path of glory that would not only make a difference to stem the judgement for a while, but at the same time ensuring receipt of their crown at the end of the race; realising that God has a personal mission for them in life. The Christian Church in this world is under constant threat from within as well as from outside. Poor teaching due to an inevitable association with worldly pleasures have left people confused and unhappy as to what it is that is required of them within their particular group. Yet the answer is simple when we examine the threat from without. Has there ever been a time where there has been so much intimidation, ranging from subtle New Age influences to positive verbal and physical attacks by religious fundamentalists of other religions? Have we not seen how the cross of Christ appears on every form of clothing to be worn blatantly by those who have little love or knowledge for what it stands for? Do we not realise exactly what satan is up to in his subtle attacks on the very things we hold dear?

When we do realise this, we begin to understand the exciting times that we live in and that we could make a very significant difference to those who are seeking and those who are lost. We could actually become part of the Grand Commission by starting slowly within our own environment, while waiting for the dynamic 'call'. We could break out and cry out to the Lord. "Please use me to make a difference. Here I am Lord."

However please be warned not to ask the Lord unless this is truly wanted, for in His mercy and grace it will be granted. The work is increasing and it would appear the workers are getting fewer. In great times of trouble and increasing apostasy, God continues to do marvellous things. Has the church been slumbering as the world slips slowly towards its ultimate destruction? No it has not. Listed below are some examples which show the Christian what the Lord has done through Godly men and women in order to bring this nation back to its God. The Church of Jesus Christ in Britain has in relatively recent times:-

1. Given Britain, Billy Graham and his Crusades
2. Allowed Mission England to take place
3. Introduced Operation 'Evangelistic Explosion'
4. Introduced Operation 'Jesus in Me.'
5. Given Reinhard Bonnke's book to every household.
6. Incredibly, allowed a postage frank to appear on millions of letters saying 'Jesus is alive!'
7. Started the 'Catch the fire' and 'Spread the fire.'

In addition to this list, every household in Britain received an invitation to join an alpha course at a local church. In this book I will not pass comment on the viability or need for each of these projects, but just want to point out the Church never slumbers. It does not matter one jot whether we believe in such activity or not, for what God leads one man to act upon He leads another away from. What does matter is what the dear Lord wants us to do about developing situations. If they are from the enemy then, at His calling, we have to act to put matters right. Everything is revealed for what it is by the Lord, but His church will struggle. The question that was asked when Bonnke's book went out to all households in the U.K. is still asked now. It is, "Are there sufficient workers in the field in order to counsel those who will respond to its contents?" Who can answer this question? All we can do individually is to tell the Lord that we are ready and available to be used at any time. For the mission field in Britain this may be a mere stepping stone for some whom the Lord will call to greater and higher things. Do we want this, or are we simply happy to let ourselves 'go with the flow'?

God is calling out the Holy Remnant, to make a stand against the battle that is waging, even though it is at present is one that may appear to some as being lost, for eventually He must come back. Judgement may have to come upon individuals and individual churches before there is a change, but this does not have to be so if they and particularly individuals seek the Lord's will. All we know is that God adds to His church every day and we all could play a part in this action. He is calling out His true church, one full of the Holy Spirit, which is ready to do battle both for the souls of the lost in the most difficult of times. Mark these words, this new church will be ridiculed and abused by the world especially within the media, however this will take place just before the judgement on Britain comes. We, as Christians can ignore the various false prophesies given today that seemingly match events, or even though we might find some disturbing and confusing, we can promise ourselves to test them and take them to heart. Jesus has warned us that many false prophets will appear at the end. (Mark 13:22) Churches may eventually be forced into practicing as little cell groups in private houses, but one thing is for sure and that is they will always exist. Persecution will eventually lead to their exponential growth.

The story in this book is about a man and a family, who said to the Lord "If you want us then take us," and that is what He did. Get excited and then ask Him. I do not like talking about myself but I must give an insight particularly to all those who wonder who on earth do I think I am to lecture people. That is to hit the nail on the head for I am no one; the point of the whole book. All I can say is that God gives wisdom to the humble and power to those who have faith, believe and want to serve. These are the only qualifications. I know there is little goodness found in me and I have to continually take my sin and problems to God and as I believe that all Christians should do this on a continual basis, I am therefore no different to any other. We have all fallen short of His glory. I will boast of my failings in order to amplify the depth and wonder of his grace, just as Paul said that he can only boast of the cross of Jesus Christ. In this we are as one.

I have my cross and I pick it up daily and because God intervenes on my behalf, time after time when my own frustrations and desperations get the better of me; I can stand and witness to His love and mercy. Very rarely does he give me what I want but he always gives me what I need, when I need it. He often gives me what I would like for other people. This could be in answered prayer or in change of situation by often supplying the funds. In this case the flow of grace is limitless providing I do not seek gain myself. I have learned that lesson the hard way. What are the riches of the world compared to all that is written in this book? It maybe that the acquisition of wealth, position, power and recognition are desirable to those in the world, but I can assure you they are the very trappings that plug grace, rot the soul and lead to perdition.

I am often thrown down but always lifted up and, true to scripture, when at my weakest he gives me His strength and the miracles abound, but is there a cost to all this? The answer is yes; a cost that few will be able to bear without being cradled in His arms. It is great, but pales into insignificance when compared to what he does in the life of a pilgrim. Besides, there is an abundance of his promises in the Bible. If believed they are nothing but stupendous. He has promised me great treasure and joy when I pass over; all this in addition to walking and ruling with him, while I live in a building more magnificent than any Bishop's palace upon this earth. The Disciple never loses sight of the Hope that is to come, in the face of want and persecution that is the now.

I have been appointed to encourage the lowest and humblest in the ranks. To reach out to whom the world would consider are dirty, easily forgotten and horrible dregs of humanity, just to say Jesus can make all the difference and that their suffering is known and there reward will be greater if He is believed and followed. Therefore I have to say that in all the days of my Christian walk, wherever I have been, the greatest amount of grace I have seen poured out has been at the bottom of the social strata, while many 'blessings' at the top, seen as Acts of God, are but curses from the devil. Is it not a wonder to people, as they check the good old bank balance every week, why God declared that the love of money is the root of all evil? Pride comes before destruction and a haughty spirit before a fall. So says our God in Proverbs 16:18.

One other factor is preeminent in my walk. Without sounding glib, I find the nearer to the bottom of the heap, the more implicit the faith, unshaken in any storm. Conversely the nearer to the 'educated top' are found those who are intellectually and theological challenged by whatever whim or fancy comes their way. I have been privileged to meet Christians living in slums, as defined by the world, in several countries on four continents and each time I have been humbled. The greatest sense of the rich blessings of the Kingdom I found amongst the Sisters charity in Calcutta. Much derided and ridiculed (as their leader), their presence in the gutters of that city illuminates everyone they come across. To see the love of Christ practically manifest its self in the foulest of conditions was life changing.

But if we do not know then how can we understand? Anyone reading this book has now been told, and after this there is no excuse for selfishness. For God's sake, His word tells us that we have to present our bodies as living sacrifices. (Romans12:1-2) Therefore my only qualification is that I have been there, I have seen it and can testify to the power of our living God. It is true. I entreat other to go and see and then tell me that I am wrong. But is this for everyone? Yes it is, as 'Calcutta' is all around us, wherever we are.

I believe that everything that has happened, and continues to happen to me is entirely due to the fact that I do my utmost to put Jesus first in all my worldly pursuits. I wear the cross of Jesus on my suit, I ask people to pray where ever I go. I have said that I have and continue to be, considered at times a complete pain in the neck. This includes family, friends and colleagues, because I bring everything down to how Jesus would see things. The important fact is that I cannot do anything else, because that is how I am led.

I do pray every day and avidly read my Bible, even though my brain can't retain it all. I try and meet with believers wherever and whenever I can. I will try and help where I can. I love praise and worship. I am no saint. I am a sinner and know my own Achilles heel(s), but I repent often and keep short accounts with the Lord. Importantly, now that I have entered the mission field in business I find that the battle is just the same. It is just as frustrating and exciting and I know that if I, with the help of my prayer partners, stay obedient then the future can only be glorious. Yet at times I get angry, I argue with my wife, I admonish my children. My daughter loves me but thinks I am doctrinally unsound on a lot of things. My eldest son has had cause to think me headstrong, but that is simply the way it is.

2008

Due to the fact that this book went to print much later than envisaged, I find it necessary to update my life simply because there is further relevant testimony. I said the cost is great if any wish to serve him as a true disciple obeying his commandments to the letter and in one sense for me worse was to follow. In the year 2000, I suffered the loss of my wife, home, business and most of my savings, because I had invested these in what was to be a Christian Retreat Centre in New Zealand. This was undoubtedly God given, because of what had to occur to make it possible. The reason why it failed are complicated, but they all add up to one thing and that was sin. God cannot be mocked and He was. It would be unbearable to rake over the coals, so I will leave the story well alone. The point of this update is to say that all the initial loss and pain that I suffered has been replaced and assuaged by a wonderful and understanding God. Where there was gleeful delight in my defeat there has been amazing victory, only possible because I took everything to Him. The Lord giveth and the Lord taketh away. (Job 1:21) I came out of this latest 'failing' with amazing discoveries of myself and closeness to Him. These are the wonderful promised compensations for loss suffered by a servant, which will lead to a strengthening of faith and power. I once again recommend a read of the book of Job. It served me well at the start of this adventure and continues to do so today.

I returned to U.K. to find that my aged mother needed a carer, and while attending to this need I also trained and entered the world of professional Caring and Child-minding. Almost immediately I was debilitated by a horrible illness which threatened to scupper everything, however I received a miraculous healing in a church that I did not frequent, having heard that a travelling South African preacher, with a healing ministry, was attending. All my family witnessed the healing and the miracles have never dried up. I am a pain in the neck to any Cessationist.

Now I am determined to enter the field of writing for only one reason and that is I have so much to tell. In this I feel that I have been given a new season of witness but now more through the pen than the mouth. Sadly as I write a whole raft of problems have hit the family and it has to be wondered why God allows this seemingly on a constant basis. It is the cost. It is the same question we all ask when our backs are against the wall. We shout 'Why me?' to our God. Is it not amazing that none of us will ever get an answer to that question! I suggest that many of the times our problems have nothing to do with God, but just life. Christians will be killed in accidents, wars, and disasters on a daily basis around the world. If we get ill, it's not because of the devil, it's not because we lack faith, it's because the guy in the same office sneezed over us. If what we believe in allows us to deal with any illness or problem then we will be fine. We are not to own it but cast it upon the yoke of Jesus, for it is easy. (Matthew 11:28-30) However should anyone be in the front line of battle for the church of Christ, then this is different as the devil may treat the servant exactly in the same way he did with Job. What a privilege that would be if we were, but it would only be with permission from the Lord. Satan cannot kill any of the faithful. If we believe that our lives are governed by Him then we cannot live or die one second earlier or later that our appointed time. He knows this and therefore if given a trial we will not be tested beyond our limits. The whole point of suffering is that we come out of it wiser. As everything is done according to His will then what have we to fear where we are, or where we go, or even what should happen? I can testify to this. I have totalled up from memory that I have nearly been killed 15 times in my life, thus far, to include bullets whizzing by either side of my head. Although the statement is a misnomer, it gives an indication that there was no way in each incident that I was anywhere near to being killed.

We can choose how we react to life threatening situations as they arise. These may include disasters during our life to when we draw our last fleeting breath. Everything is handed to Him because He is love. The Bible says this casts out all fear and through experience I concur. Grace will follow and the recipient will see a return of power and miracles. Our problem is fear, but the Bible deals with this in a wonderful way.

'There is no fear in love. But perfect love drives out fear, because fear has to do with punishment. The one who fears is not made perfect in love.'
(1 John14:18)

Jesus said.

"If you love me you will obey what I command."
(John 14:15)

Regarding failure, well it is now easy for us to admit that we all fail often in our Christian walk. In fact most of our lives consist of total failure and a person only needs to have brought up children to understand the validity of this statement. In life most of what we panic over seems utterly unimportant later on. Meetings after meetings seem to go the same way. What did we achieve? However, if we try to do our best for and with Jesus as our mentor, then not only does he accept all we do, but will constantly encourage us to move forward via another little test. He gives us glimpses of the way and then provides us with the tools to get the job done. He then will clear up all the mess we make which gives us a hope for the future, where we lack wisdom. Is it just possible that these are the ingredients for success and not failure?

I would like to include with one final thought from the book of Romans where the Apostle Paul quotes ancient scripture. It should be tucked away for consideration every time we speak to someone.

'Those who were not told about him will see, and those who have not heard will understand.'
(Romans 15:7)

Failing for Jesus does not make one a failure, it just makes one stronger.

ND - #0245 - 080726 - C0 - 197/132/18 - PB - 9781780357942 - Gloss Lamination